Los Angeles Dodgers IQ

THE ULTIMATE TEST OF TRUE FANDOM

Copyright © 2018 Tucker Elliot.

All rights reserved.

ISBN: 978-0-9912699-1-4

Cover design by Holly Walden Ross.

Front cover photo courtesy of Mark Whitt. Back cover photo courtesy of Russel Tiffin.

Interior layout and formatting by BMP Digital.

Black Mesa

Florida

CONTENTS

	INTRODUCTION	i
1	THE NUMBERS GAME	1
2	BASEBALL QUOTES	13
3	FRANCHISE RECORDS	23
4	OCTOBER BASEBALL	35
5	THE SLUGGERS	49
6	THE HURLERS	59
7	FANTASTIC FEATS	71
8	AWARD WINNERS	83
9	THE TEAMS	95
10	EXTRA INNINGS	107

INTRODUCTION

Arthur Daley, the Pulitzer Prize-winning sportswriter for the *New York Times*, wrote more than eleven thousand daily columns and twenty million words covering sports all over the world—but his favorite sport was baseball, and on that subject he famously wrote, "A baseball fan has the digestive apparatus of a billy goat. He can, and does, devour any set of statistics with insatiable appetite and then nuzzles hungrily for more."

Daley was right, of course.

Baseball relies on numbers and statistics more than any other sport—and we use those numbers to measure success and failure, they guide our decisions in playing and managing the game, they fuel our discussions when watching the game as a spectator or reliving it over the water cooler at work, and they keep us awake late at night, celebrating or lamenting, depending on, well, the final score.

Numbers, for the most part, don't lie.

Statistics on the other hand … well, it depends who you ask. Bob Woolf was a Boston lawyer and a pioneer in the business of representing athletes in contract negotiations and sponsorship deals. In other words, he was one of the first sports agents. Woolf related this anecdote about Boston Red Sox pitcher Bob Stanley: "When I negotiated his contract with the Red Sox, we had statistics demonstrating he was the third best pitcher in the league. They had a chart showing he was the sixtieth best pitcher in the Red Sox organization." Perhaps it's the ability to manipulate and interpret statistics that makes numbers so fascinating to baseball fans.

Here's what I know about baseball and numbers that is incontrovertible: math was my favorite grade school subject because it was the easiest. I knew it already from calculating batting averages and earned run averages and projecting how many hits and RBIs I'd have at the end of the season based on the games I'd already played—math skills that were easily three or four years ahead of my grade level at the time. My mom was the official scorekeeper at our Little League games and we'd spend hours each week pouring through the scorebook, tabulating all the stats, and then placing them in columns and charts on construction paper as if it was the back of my very own Topps baseball card.

Numbers resonate with baseball fans, no question about it.

It's not just the stats, either. We use numbers to track the performance of our favorite players, sure, but we also use numbers to identify them—as in jersey numbers. I met Johnny Bench once during spring training. Big surprise—I wore #5 a few weeks later when my summer league kicked off. You can track my idols using my Little League and high school jersey numbers: #5 (Bench), #8 (Gary Carter), #23 (Don Mattingly), and #8 again (Cal Ripken Jr.). There's a very good reason why franchises retire jersey numbers to honor their most important stars—just as a fan wearing a #22 Dodgers tee shirt is making a statement about Clayton Kershaw's contributions to the club, when the club retires a number it's making a statement about that player's significance to the history of the entire organization.

This is a book of trivia, but it is derived from numbers.

And collectively they tell the story of the Los Angeles Dodgers.

Now step up to the plate.

Challenge yourself.

Enjoy, and reminisce.

This is your Los Angeles Dodgers IQ, the ultimate test of true fandom.

"It's time for Dodger baseball!"
— *Vin Scully*

1 THE NUMBERS GAME

Any self-respecting fan should be able to cite the most notable and historic stats in franchise history—and you should also be able to identify the most revered jersey numbers in franchise history. Dodger history is replete with superstars and individuals who distinguished themselves as fan-favorites, and that's why we open the top of the first with a simple numbers game: do you know the jersey numbers for these all-time greats?

TOP OF THE FIRST

Q1: Jackie Robinson is an American icon whose life and career transcends baseball and continues to inspire new generations of fans. The Dodgers retired his #42 jersey on June 4, 1972—and decades later every current major-league team took the extraordinary step of retiring #42 in honor of Jackie Robinson's legacy of courage. What year did every MLB team retire Robinson's #42?
    a) 1997
    b) 2004
    c) 2007
    d) 2012

Q2: Roy Campanella had a five-year stretch in which he won three league MVP Awards and led the Dodgers to victory in the 1955 World Series. The Hall of Fame legend was an All-Star eight times in 10 seasons before his career was tragically cut short by a car accident that left him paralyzed. What is the number retired by the Dodgers in honor of Roy Campanella?
    a) 9
    b) 19
    c) 29
    d) 39

Q3: The Dodgers' website at MLB.com calls Sandy Koufax "[one of] the most dominating pitchers in the game's history." In 12 seasons he won three Cy Young Awards, one league MVP Award, and two World Series MVP Awards. What is the number retired by the Dodgers in honor of Sandy Koufax?
    a) 2
    b) 12
    c) 22
    d) 32

Q4: Don Drysdale was a hard-throwing righty who pitched for five pennant-winning teams and led three of them to victory in the World Series. Drysdale is best known for his consecutive scoreless innings streak in 1968—but by that point in his career he'd already won a Cy Young Award and led the league in strikeouts three times. What is the number retired by the Dodgers in honor of Don Drysdale?
  a) 43
  b) 47
  c) 53
  d) 57

Q5: Don Sutton debuted with the Dodgers in 1966 and would go on to play 16 of 23 big-league seasons in Los Angeles during two stints with the club. He was a consistent winner throughout his career and as a result was elected to the Hall of Fame in 1998. Sutton's pitching contributed to three pennants for the Dodgers and another for the Milwaukee Brewers—but it was simply bad luck that his teams lost the World Series all four times. Sutton was also on the 1986 California Angels club that lost the ALCS in heartbreaking fashion to the Boston Red Sox—and he was on the 1988 Dodgers club that won the World Series by shocking the heavily favored Oakland Athletics … but unfortunately he was released by the Dodgers in August of that season and missed out on the championship. Nonetheless … he's a Dodger legend. What is the number retired by the Dodgers in honor of Don Sutton?
  a) 15
  b) 20
  c) 25
  d) 30

Q6: Walter Alston is etched forever in franchise history for guiding the club to its first world championship in 1955. Alston was a longtime minor league skipper when the club hired him in 1954, but he was a virtual unknown at the big-league level. No worries. The club won 92 games his first season and 98 on its way to the World Series a year later. What is the number retired by the Dodgers in honor of Walter Alston?

    a) 4
    b) 14
    c) 24
    d) 34

Q7: Jim Gilliam is the only player not in the Hall of Fame to have his number retired by the Dodgers. After beginning his career in the Negro Leagues he signed with the Dodgers in 1951 and debuted two years later. Gilliam won seven pennants and four world championships during 14 seasons in Brooklyn and Los Angeles. He later coached for the Dodgers and was on the staff of three more pennant-winning teams before his untimely death just two days before the Dodgers took the field in Game 1 of the 1978 World Series. The club retired his number prior to that game. What is the number retired by the Dodgers in honor of Jim Gilliam?

    a) 9
    b) 19
    c) 29
    d) 39

Q8: Walter Alston might have been an unknown when he took the helm in LA but he was a legend by the time he left—and it was Tommy Lasorda who had the daunting task of following Alston's footsteps. Alston and Lasorda had at least two things in common—the first was an undistinguished career as a player (Alston batted just once in the big-leagues and struck out, and Lasorda appeared in just 26 big-league games as a pitcher) and the second was that it was the Dodgers who were willing to take a chance on each man as a manager. Well, it worked out—both are in the Hall of Fame, both found immediate success, and both sustained that success over the long term. What is the number retired by the Dodgers in honor of Tommy Lasorda?

    a) 2
    b) 4
    c) 8
    d) 12

Q9: The Dodgers' website at MLB.com calls Duke Snider one of baseball's "most feared hitters" during the 16 seasons he played in Brooklyn and LA. He was a seven-time All-Star in center field and he led the Dodgers to six pennants and two world championships. What is the number retired by the Dodgers in honor of Duke Snider?

    a) 2
    b) 4
    c) 8
    d) 12

Q10: Known as "The Little Colonel," Pee Wee Reese was a 10-time All-Star and team captain who played for seven pennant-winning teams in Brooklyn. The Hall of Fame legend had his number retired by the Dodgers in 1984. What is the number retired by the Dodgers in honor of Pee Wee Reese?

    a) 1
    b) 7
    c) 11
    d) 17

TOP OF THE FIRST
ANSWER KEY

1: a. 1997.

2: d. 39.

3: d. 32.

4: c. 53.

5: b. 20.

6: c. 24.

7: b. 19.

8: a. 2.

9: b. 4.

10: a. 1.

LOS ANGELES DODGERS IQ

BOTTOM OF THE FIRST

Q11: Fernando Valenzuela was a 20-year-old rookie when he took the baseball world by storm in 1981. The lefty from Mexico led the league in complete games, shutouts, innings and strikeouts on his way to winning Cy Young and Rookie of the Year honors … and the 1981 World Series. What jersey number did Fernando Valenzuela wear during 11 seasons pitching for the Dodgers?
    a) 14
    b) 24
    c) 34
    d) 44

Q12: Kirk Gibson played just three seasons in LA but with one swing in October he gave Dodgers fans one of the greatest moments in baseball history. Gibson's home run vs. Dennis Eckersley to win Game 1 of the 1988 World Series couldn't have been scripted any better by a Hollywood screenwriter. What jersey number did Kirk Gibson wear during his time with the Dodgers?
    a) 23
    b) 25
    c) 30
    d) 33

Q13: Steve Sax was a 21-year-old kid when he debuted for the Dodgers in August 1981. He wore #52 while playing 31 games that year—and he played well enough that he was also included on the club's postseason roster. One year later Sax was a star wearing a different jersey number on his way to earning Rookie of the Year honors. What jersey number did Steve Sax wear during seven seasons with the Dodgers from 1982-88?
    a) 3
    b) 6

c) 7
d) 9

Q14: Davey Lopes was drafted at the relatively late age of twenty-three and he was twenty-seven by the time he debuted for the Dodgers in 1972. It didn't matter. He was a base-stealing machine and the second baseman for a Dodgers infield featuring Steve Garvey, Bill Russell, and Ron Cey that took the field together every season from 1974-81. What jersey number did Davey Lopes wear during 10 seasons with the Dodgers from 1972-81?
  a) 11
  b) 13
  c) 15
  d) 17

Q15: Mike Scioscia was never fleet of foot. It was Tommy Lasorda who said, "If he raced his pregnant wife he'd finish third." (In fairness to Scioscia, Lasorda used those exact words to describe a number of players over the years.) As the Dodgers catcher, however, Scioscia was a two-time All-Star and a world champion who built a reputation for being one of the game's best at blocking the plate and tagging out base runners who *were* fast. What jersey number did Mike Scioscia wear during 13 seasons with the Dodgers from 1980-92?
  a) 4
  b) 14
  c) 24
  d) 34

Q16: Mike Piazza is famous for many things, most notably as one of the most prolific offensive catchers in baseball history and for his World Series confrontation with Roger Clemens—but early on he was known as the guy selected in the 62nd-round of the 1988 draft as a favor to Piazza's dad, who was friends with Tommy Lasorda. There were 1,390 players drafted ahead of him but it was Piazza who just

five years later won 1993 NL Rookie of the Year honors and the first of six consecutive Silver Slugger Awards. Piazza wore #25 during his 21-game cup of coffee in 1992. What jersey number did he wear during five full seasons with the Dodgers from 1993-97?
  a) 31
  b) 32
  c) 33
  d) 34

Q17: Eric Karros was an economics major at UCLA who decided to walk-on with the baseball team. Good move. That led to the Dodgers drafting him in the sixth-round of the 1988 draft—some 1,250 picks ahead of Mike Piazza—and four years later he was the 1992 NL Rookie of the Year. What jersey number did Eric Karros wear during 12 seasons with the Dodgers from 1991-2002?
  a) 18
  b) 23
  c) 32
  d) 38

Q18: Pedro Guerrero toiled in the minor leagues for most of the 1970s (he started rookie ball as a 17-year-old kid in 1973), but by 1980 he was a permanent fixture in the Dodgers lineup and for the rest of the decade he was one of the most feared hitters in baseball. He wore #57 during 30 games with the Dodgers in 1978-79. What jersey number did Pedro Guerrero wear during nine seasons with the Dodgers from 1980-88?
  a) 8
  b) 18
  c) 28
  d) 38

Q19: Steve Garvey was a slick-fielding first baseman who could flat-out hit—in a span of seven seasons he had 200-plus hits six times, and he had 192 hits in the one season he came up short. Garvey was a Gold Glove winner, league MVP and world champion with the Dodgers. What jersey number did Steve Garvey wear during parts of 14 seasons with the club from 1969-82?

    a) 4
    b) 5
    c) 6
    d) 7

Q20: Orel Hershiser spent parts of 18 seasons in the big-leagues but it was a single season—1988—that forever etched his name in baseball lore. In addition to his record-setting 59 consecutive scoreless innings, Hershiser won a Cy Young, Gold Glove, NLCS MVP, and World Series MVP as the Dodgers defeated the Oakland Athletics in the Fall Classic. What jersey number did Orel Hershiser wear during two stints and 14 seasons with the club from 1983-2000?

    a) 52
    b) 53
    c) 54
    d) 55

LOS ANGELES DODGERS IQ

BOTTOM OF THE FIRST
ANSWER KEY

11: c. 34.

12: a. 23.

13: a. 3.

14: c. 15.

15: b. 14.

16: a. 31.

17: b. 23.

18: c. 28.

19: c. 6.

20: d. 55.

"You've gotta win. And if you don't win … you'll fall by the wayside. And to tell you how bad I want to win, a few years ago we were playing in Cincinnati. I got up Sunday morning and I went to church and who came in and sat right next to me was the manager of the Cincinnati Reds, Johnny McNamara. Now, I knew why I was in church. And *he* knew why I was there … he knelt down and he lit a candle … and when he left, I went down and I blew that candle out! I knew one thing. He was *not* lighting that candle for a dead relative."

— *Tommy Lasorda*

2 BASEBALL QUOTES

No other sport inspires quotes like baseball. Dozens of books are out there filled with nothing but quotes from the game's great players, managers, umpires, writers, and broadcasters. One reason we're fascinated with baseball quotes is because they tell us the history of the game in the words of those who were there to make or witness firsthand the plays that inspired generations of fans. Baseball has inspired more written words than any other sport—and many of the legends who inspired those words played their home games at Dodger Stadium.

Plus, we have Tommy Lasorda and Vin Scully.

How lucky are we?

We begin the second with trivia inspired by our love for baseball quotes—do you know which Dodgers these words were spoken about?

TOP OF THE SECOND

Q21: Jim Murray said of this legend: "[He's] the only guy in the game who could look Billy Graham right in the face without blushing and who would order corn on the cob in a Paris Restaurant."
    a) Roy Campanella
    b) Walter Alston
    c) Duke Snider
    d) Pee Wee Reese

Q22: This legend said in his Hall of Fame induction speech: "When you love a game like this, you're not worrying about your paychecks on the first and fifteenth … I know, I played nine years for nothing."
    a) Roy Campanella
    b) Jackie Robinson
    c) Pee Wee Reese
    d) Don Drysdale

Q23: Dick Groat, who won the 1960 NL batting title and MVP Award, said about this Dodgers pitcher: "Batting against [him] is the same as making a date with a dentist."
    a) Sandy Koufax
    b) Don Sutton
    c) Don Drysdale
    d) Hoyt Wilhelm

Q24: Baseball icon Yogi Berra once said of this Dodgers pitcher: "I can see how he won 25 games. What I don't understand is how he lost five."
    a) Fernando Valenzuela
    b) Don Drysdale
    c) Don Sutton
    d) Sandy Koufax

Q25: Danny Ozark, who spent eight years on Walter Alston's coaching staff before taking over managerial duties for the Phillies, said of this Dodgers manager: "[He] was a great motivator. He treated his players and coaches tremendously, and everyone on the team would do anything for him."
  a) Leo Durocher
  b) Tommy Lasorda
  c) Casey Stengel
  d) Burleigh Grimes

Q26: This Dodger legend, who was known as a great leader and for being a great teammate, once said: "If you rush in and out of the clubhouse, you rush in and out of baseball."
  a) Pee Wee Reese
  b) Duke Snider
  c) Sandy Koufax
  d) Steve Garvey

Q27: Roger Kahn, author of the classic book *The Boys of Summer*, said of this player: "He could hit and bunt and steal and run. He had intimidating skills, and he burned with a dark fire."
  a) Willie Keeler
  b) Maury Wills
  c) Jackie Robinson
  d) Willie Davis

Q28: This Dodger legend once said: "What a player does best, he should practice least. Practice is for problems."
  a) Gil Hodges
  b) Duke Snider
  c) Roy Campanella
  d) Steve Garvey

Q29: Tommy Lasorda said of this pitcher: "When you gave him the

ball, you knew one thing—your pitcher was going to give you everything he had."
   a) Fernando Valenzuela
   b) Bob Welch
   c) Orel Hershiser
   d) Don Sutton

Q30: This baseball icon once said: "Andre Dawson has a bruised knee and is listed as day-to-day … *aren't we all?*"
   a) Vin Scully
   b) Jerry Doggett
   c) Ross Porter
   d) Rick Monday

TOP OF THE SECOND
ANSWER KEY

21: b. Walter Alston.

22: a. Roy Campanella.

23: c. Don Drysdale.

24: d. Sandy Koufax.

25: b. Tommy Lasorda.

26: a. Pee Wee Reese.

27: c. Jackie Robinson.

28: b. Duke Snider.

29: d. Don Sutton.

30: a. Vin Scully.

BOTTOM OF THE SECOND

Q31: Vin Scully said of this player: "[He] could wake up on Christmas morning and hit a line drive to center." Adding to that thought, sportswriter Jim Murray said of this same player: "You could wake [him] up at 2am, hand him a toothpick, throw an aspirin tablet toward him, and he would hit it for a line drive single to right."
  a) Bill Russell
  b) Maury Wills
  c) Davey Lopes
  d) Manny Mota

Q32: Bill James, one of the most influential writers and statisticians in baseball thanks to his scientific approach to studying the game, once called this slugger: "The best hitter God has made in a long time."
  a) Pedro Guerrero
  b) Matt Kemp
  c) Eric Karros
  d) Mike Piazza

Q33: This legendary manager, known for his competitive spirit, is credited with such statements as: "As long as I've got a chance to beat you I'm going to take it" and "Buy a steak for a player on another club after the game, but don't even speak to him on the field … get out there and beat him to death."
  a) Casey Stengel
  b) Leo Durocher
  c) Walter Alston
  d) Tommy Lasorda

Q34: Tommy Lasorda could deliver off-the-cuff good-natured quips about his players better than anybody. He once said of this pitcher:

"Last year we tried to teach him English and the only word he learned was million."
 a) Fernando Valenzuela
 b) Chan Ho Park
 c) Hideo Nomo
 d) Ramon Martinez

Q35: This fiery pitcher displayed his attitude toward hitters—both opponents and teammates—with statements such as: "I hate all hitters ... I start a game mad and I stay that way until it's over" and "If they knocked two of your guys down, I'd get four ... you have to protect your hitters."
 a) Don Newcombe
 b) Phil Regan
 c) Don Drysdale
 d) Ron Perranoski

Q36: This legendary pitcher demonstrated what made him so great with statements such as: "Pitching is the art of instilling fear" and "Show me a guy who can't pitch inside and I'll show you a loser."
 a) Sandy Koufax
 b) Don Sutton
 c) Don Drysdale
 d) Fernando Valenzuela

Q37: This player's passion for the game is evident in this oft-quoted statement: "I never want to quit playing ball. They'll have to cut this uniform off of me to get me out of it."
 a) Duke Snider
 b) Roy Campanella
 c) Jackie Robinson
 d) Steve Yeager

Q38: This iconic Dodger captain once said: "Being captain of the

Dodgers meant representing an organization committed to winning and trying to keep it going. We could have won every year if the breaks had gone right."
   a) Duke Snider
   b) Maury Wills
   c) Davey Lopes
   d) Pee Wee Reese

Q39: This legend expressed the following sentiment with both his words and actions: "A life is not important except in the impact it has on other lives."
   a) Roy Campanella
   b) Jackie Robinson
   c) Walter Alston
   d) Tommy Lasorda

Q40: Long after his own playing career ended, this Dodger legend made the following observation about contemporary players: "Man, if I made a million dollars I'd come in at six in the morning, sweep the stands, wash the uniforms, clean out the office, manage the team *and* play the games."
   a) Sandy Koufax
   b) Don Drysdale
   c) Duke Snider
   d) Pee Wee Reese

BOTTOM OF THE SECOND
ANSWER KEY

31: d. Manny Mota.

32: a. Pedro Guerrero.

33: b. Leo Durocher.

34: a. Fernando Valenzuela.

35: c. Don Drysdale.

36: a. Sandy Koufax.

37: b. Roy Campanella.

38: d. Pee Wee Reese.

39: b. Jackie Robinson.

40: c. Duke Snider.

"You can't get real happy or real depressed when you play baseball—it's a great sport in that it offers a player a lot of opportunities for atonement."
— *Mike Piazza*

3 FRANCHISE RECORDS

It's impossible to tell the story of major-league baseball without the Dodgers ... because so much of baseball history was made by the Dodgers. The record books are filled with guys in Blue.

Regular season. Postseason. It doesn't matter.

Blue.

The biggest names in baseball.

Here in the third, we explore some of the most significant franchise records and relive moments from some of the biggest names in the game.

TOP OF THE THIRD

Q41: The 1953 Brooklyn Dodgers won 105 games to claim the NL pennant by 13 1/2 games over the Milwaukee Braves. That victory total set a club record for the Brooklyn era in franchise history. The 2017 pennant-winning Dodgers set a club record for the LA era in franchise history. How many games did the Dodgers win in 2017?
    a) 101
    b) 102
    c) 103
    d) 104

Q42: Brooklyn ran away with the pennant in 1953 thanks to a record-setting performance at home: the Dodgers were an incredible 60-17 at Ebbets Field, the highest home wins total in franchise history. In 2017, it was once again home-field success that fueled LA. The 2017 Dodgers won the most home games of any team in LA history. What was the home won-loss record for the Dodgers in 2017?
    a) 55-26
    b) 56-25
    c) 57-24
    d) 58-23

Q43: Two players spent a franchise record 18 seasons with the club—one did it in Brooklyn, the other in LA. Which two players share this remarkable record?
    a) Zack Wheat/Willie Davis
    b) Pee Wee Reese/Bill Russell
    c) Zack Wheat/Bill Russell
    d) Pee Wee Reese/Willie Davis

Q44: Willie Keeler holds the franchise record with a .352 career batting average during four-plus seasons in Brooklyn around the turn

of the 20th century. The highest career average for a player with at least 1,500 plate appearances for the LA Dodgers is .331. Who set this record?
a) Gary Sheffield
b) Manny Mota
c) Mike Piazza
d) Pedro Guerrero

Q45: Babe Herman played seven seasons with the club in Brooklyn and he had an extraordinary run in 1929-30 that saw him post these ridiculous numbers: .381 average, 105 runs, 217 hits, 42 doubles, 21 home runs, and 113 RBIs in 1929; and .393 average, 143 runs, 241 hits, 48 doubles, 35 home runs, and 130 RBIs in 1930. And the really ridiculous part ... *none of those stats led the NL.* Herman did manage to record the two highest season averages in franchise history. From 1958-2017 the highest season average by a player for the LA Dodgers was .362. Who set this record?
a) Gary Sheffield
b) Manny Mota
c) Mike Piazza
d) Pedro Guerrero

Q46: This one might be a bit surprising. The franchise leader for career slugging percentage never led the league in that category despite 22 seasons in the majors and a career .514 slugging percentage. In more than 2,000 career plate appearances with the Dodgers his slugging percentage was a franchise-best .573. Who holds this record?
a) Gary Sheffield
b) Shawn Green
c) Raul Mondesi
d) Ron Cey

Q47: Gil Hodges, Bill Russell, Pee Wee Reese, and Zack Wheat are

the only players from any era in franchise history to play more than 2,000 games with the Dodgers. Who played in a franchise record 2,322 games for the club?
a) Gil Hodges
b) Bill Russell
c) Pee Wee Reese
d) Zack Wheat

Q48: Among the more impressive feats a player can perform over the course of a season is to play in every one of his club's games. Thanks to the best-of-three divisional playoff in 1962—which counted as regular season games—Maury Wills is the only player in franchise history to play a record 165 regular games in a single season … but is he also the only player in team history to play 162 or more games in a season a record six times? Who did this for the Dodgers?
a) Maury Wills
b) Steve Garvey
c) Tommy Davis
d) Bill Russell

Q49: In 1890, Hub Collins scored a franchise record 148 runs for the Brooklyn Dodgers. Babe Herman's 143 runs in 1930 is the highest total in the modern era. The highest season total in the LA era is 130. Who is the only player to score 130 runs in a season for the Dodgers from 1958-2017?
a) Duke Snider
b) Maury Wills
c) Shawn Green
d) Rafael Furcal

Q50: Among players who played exclusively during the LA era of franchise history, who scored a record 876 runs for the Dodgers?
a) Bill Russell
b) Steve Garvey

c) Maury Wills
d) Davey Lopes

TOP OF THE THIRD
ANSWER KEY

41: b. 102.

42: c. 57-24.

43: c. Zack Wheat/Bill Russell.

44: c. Mike Piazza.

45: c. Mike Piazza.

46: a. Gary Sheffield.

47: d. Zack Wheat.

48: b. Steve Garvey.

49: b. Maury Wills.

50: c. Maury Wills.

BOTTOM OF THE THIRD

Q51: In 1930, Babe Herman set a franchise record with 241 hits. In 1953, Roy Campanella set a franchise record with a league-best 142 RBIs. And then this player … in one season he set an LA era franchise record with 230 hits and surpassed Campanella in the record book with 153 RBIs on his way to winning two-thirds of the Triple Crown. Who set these lofty standards for the Dodgers?
a) Steve Garvey
b) Duke Snider
c) Tommy Davis
d) Shawn Green

Q52: Duke Snider hit 40-plus home runs in five consecutive seasons from 1953-57. No one else in franchise history has more than two 40-homer seasons—and only two players aside from Snider have done that: Gil Hodges did it for Brooklyn in 1951 and 1954, and then this player did it after the club moved west to LA … who is he?
a) Steve Garvey
b) Shawn Green
c) Mike Piazza
d) Gary Sheffield

Q53: Duke Snider had just 15 home runs in 1958, the Dodgers first year out west, for his lowest full season total at that point in his career—and he never hit more than 23 after the club moved to LA. It actually took quite a while before the Dodgers had a 40-homer guy in LA. Who was the first player with a 40-homer season for the LA Dodgers?
a) Steve Garvey
b) Shawn Green
c) Mike Piazza
d) Gary Sheffield

Q54: Duke Snider is the franchise leader with 389 career home runs—but among the sluggers who have played exclusively in LA, who hit a franchise record 270 bombs for the Dodgers?
a) Eric Karros
b) Ron Cey
c) Mike Piazza
d) Steve Garvey

Q55: Bob Caruthers won 40 games for the Brooklyn Bridegrooms in 1889. That mark is a franchise record for all eras—but if you look only at the modern era (since 1900) there have only been two pitchers who won as many as 28 games in a season: Hall of Famers Joe McGinnity (1900) and Dazzy Vance (1924). The franchise record for the LA era is 27. Who holds this mark?
a) Don Newcombe
b) Sandy Koufax
c) Don Drysdale
d) Don Sutton

Q56: No one won more games for the Dodgers than Hall of Fame legend Don Sutton—his 233 wins is easily a franchise record and it remains unthreatened more than a quarter-century after he last pitched in the majors. Only one other pitcher has won more than 200 games for the Dodgers. Who else aside from Sutton has this distinction?
a) Sandy Koufax
b) Orel Hershiser
c) Don Drysdale
d) Don Newcombe

Q57: Who is the franchise leader for career innings and strikeouts?
a) Don Drysdale
b) Sandy Koufax
c) Don Sutton

d) Dazzy Vance

Q58: In 1963, the Dodgers had an astounding 20 shutouts on the season. LA blanked 13 teams at home—which means better than 1-in-4 of the club's home wins were shutouts. Sandy Koufax led the way. He set a franchise record with 11 shutouts. To put that into perspective … the entire San Francisco Giants pitching staff had nine shutouts in 1963. But is Koufax the franchise leader for career shutouts? Who pitched a record 52 shutouts for the Dodgers?
   a) Don Drysdale
   b) Sandy Koufax
   c) Don Sutton
   d) Dazzy Vance

Q59: This relief pitcher appeared in an astounding 106 games in a single season to set a major-league record … and he also set records that same year for pitching 208 innings and earning 27 decisions out of the bullpen. For his efforts he was the first relief pitcher in history to win the Cy Young Award. Who had such a remarkable year for the Dodgers?
   a) Eric Gagne
   b) Charlie Hough
   c) Ron Perranoski
   d) Mike Marshall

Q60: From 1958-2017, there were 20 pitchers with at least 100 decisions and 1,000 innings for the Los Angeles Dodgers. The list is a who's who of Hall of Famers and Cy Young winners, but also includes All-Stars and fan-favorites such as Chan Ho Park, Hideo Nomo, Chad Billingsley, and Ramon Martinez. It's an impressive club, to be sure—and one of its members has the lowest earned run average in Los Angeles Dodgers history. Who holds this impressive record?
   a) Sandy Koufax

b) Clayton Kershaw
c) Don Drysdale
d) Orel Hershiser

BOTTOM OF THE THIRD
ANSWER KEY

51: c. Tommy Davis.

52: b. Shawn Green.

53: c. Mike Piazza.

54: a. Eric Karros.

55: b. Sandy Koufax.

56: c. Don Drysdale.

57: c. Don Sutton.

58: c. Don Sutton.

59: d. Mike Marshall.

60: b. Clayton Kershaw.

"High fly ball into right field, she is … gone! In a year that has been so improbable, the impossible has happened!"
— *Vin Scully*

4 OCTOBER BASEBALL

"Next year" is the mentality that 29 of baseball's 30 teams cling to each winter, for there can be only one winner—as the 2017 Dodgers are painfully aware.

In the spring, the wins column is reset.

Last season is history.

And the goal is the same for every club: October baseball.

The journey is 162 games long, and the destination is a chance for baseball immortality. Kirk Gibson knows a thing or two about that. As does Orel Hershiser, Sandy Koufax, Steve Yeager, Ron Cey, Pedro Guerrero, Larry Sherry and Johnny Podres. On to the fourth, and a look at Dodgers in the postseason.

TOP OF THE FOURTH

Q61: Bob Costas opened NBC's broadcast of Game 1 of the 1988 World Series by saying, "First item of business: Kirk Gibson will not play tonight." Later, as the Dodgers trailed the Oakland Athletics 4-3 in the eighth, the NBC cameras panned the dugout but Gibson was noticeably absent. Vin Scully then said, "There is no Gibson. The man who was the spearhead of the Dodger offense throughout the year, who saved them in the league championship series, will not see any action tonight, for sure. He is not even in the dugout." Of course Gibson did save the Dodgers that night with one of the most memorable and clutch home runs in baseball history … but only because a former Athletics outfielder made it possible. Who pinch-hit for the Dodgers against his former team—despite a .196 average during the regular season—and drew a two-out walk to set up Gibson's game-winning blast?
   a) Danny Heep
   b) Mike Davis
   c) Jose Gonzalez
   d) Mike Sharperson

Q62: Kirk Gibson's dramatic pinch-hit home run vs. Dennis Eckersley was voted "the greatest moment in LA sports history" in a 1995 poll. A's shortstop Walt Weiss had no problem with that. A decade after the Dodgers upset his Oakland Athletics in the World Series, Weiss told *Sporting News*, "As devastating a blow as it was, I remember running off the field and saying, 'Man, that was unbelievable.'" Not everyone in the A's dugout that night shares Weiss' sentiment. This player/coach has publicly stated that he refuses to watch the video clip of Gibson's home run anytime it's played on TV or in a stadium montage. He also said, "I knew it was gone, and I got very vulgar about it in the dugout." Who made these statements?

a) Tony La Russa
b) Dave Duncan
c) Dave Stewart
d) Jose Canseco

Q63: Kirk Gibson and Tommy Lasorda are quick to give credit to the Dodgers scouting department for their role in Gibson's game-winning home run. A's ace closer Dennis Eckersley had walked only 11 batters the entire season, and only 21 of 279 batters he faced managed to work a full count against the 1988 AL Cy Young runner-up—but a member of the scouting department was so thorough in his report that he told the club's left handed hitters, "Don't ever forget this, if you're up in the ninth inning and we're down or it's tied and you get to three-and-two against Eckersley—partner, sure as I'm standing here breathing, you're going to see a backdoor slider." And of course it was a three-and-two backdoor slider that Gibson launched majestically into the right field seats. Whose sage advice did Gibson recall in his historic at-bat vs. Eckersley?
a) Jerry Stephenson
b) Ralph Avila
c) Steve Boros
d) Mel Didier

Q64: Almost as unbelievable as Kirk Gibson's bomb was the two-run shot by Gibson's fill-in starter against Oakland's 21-game winner Dave Stewart. This part-time outfielder hit only one home run during the regular season, but he went deep in the first World Series at-bat of his career to give LA an early lead. The home run was so unexpected that Tommy Lasorda said, "God must have said let's gift him a home run and let this happen." Who started in place of an injured Kirk Gibson during Game 1 of the 1988 World Series?
a) Danny Heep
b) Mike Davis

c) Mickey Hatcher
d) Mike Devereaux

Q65: Reggie Jackson pummeled the Dodgers with five home runs during the final three games of the 1977 World Series—including three in the decisive Game 6—and when LA and New York met again in the 1978 World Series, the Yankees' slugger wasted no time going yard again. "Mr. October" made it six home runs over his last four World Series games against LA with a Game 1 blast at Dodger Stadium. But in a critical moment in Game 2, it was a 21-year-old Dodger rookie who outshone Jackson in the spotlight. Who struck out Reggie Jackson on a three-two fastball with two outs and two on in the ninth inning of a 4-3 Dodger victory?
a) Bob Welch
b) Rick Sutcliffe
c) Dave Stewart
d) Bobby Castillo

Q66: Hall of Fame legend Nolan Ryan pitched a complete-game two-hitter to put the Dodgers into a one-game hole in the best-of-five 1981 NLDS. LA lost Game 2 as well, but battled back to even the series with back-to-back wins in Games 3 and 4 … only to face Ryan again in the decisive Game 5. Ryan had posted 11 wins against 5 losses during the strike-shortened season, and the flamethrower had his best stuff all year on the way to a league and career best 1.69 earned run average. However, this far less heralded pitcher took the mound for LA and outpitched the iconic Ryan Express. Rick Monday broke a scoreless tie in the sixth and Ryan was knocked from the game, while the Dodgers starter went on to pitch a complete-game shutout as the club advanced to the NLCS. Who bested Ryan in Game 5 of the 1981 NLDS with one of the most clutch performances in franchise history?
a) Burt Hooton

b) Jerry Reuss
c) Bob Welch
d) Fernando Valenzuela

Q67: After rallying to beat the Astros, the 1981 Dodgers won the NLCS in dramatic fashion vs. the Montreal Expos. With the series tied two games apiece, Fernando Valenzuela and Bob Welch combined on a three-hitter in the decisive Game 5 as the Dodgers held on for a 2-1 last at-bat victory and a date with the Yankees in the World Series. And the last at-bat game-winner? It was a bomb. Who won the 1981 pennant with a home run?
   a) Dusty Baker
   b) Steve Garvey
   c) Ron Cey
   d) Rick Monday

Q68: The 1981 World Series was the third time in five seasons that the LA Dodgers met the New York Yankees in the World Series, and it was also the third time in franchise history that the Dodgers beat the Yankees to claim the title world champions. No other teams in history have met in the World Series as many times as the Dodgers and Yankees. What is the record number of times the Fall Classic has been a Dodgers vs. Yankees affair?
   a) 10
   b) 11
   c) 12
   d) 13

Q69: After a nine-year drought, the Dodgers claimed the 2004 NL West title with one of the most improbable rallies in franchise history. LA trailed San Francisco 3-0 in the bottom of the ninth on the second to last day of the season. A win would secure the title for the Dodgers, a loss would send the title chase to the season's final day. The inning began with a single and a walk, but then a strikeout threatened to quell the rally. Only the Giants couldn't get another out as a walk, walk, E6, and another single set the stage for a walk-off grand slam. The guy who hit it would later say he was looking for a pitch that he could get some lift and drive home the winning run with a sacrifice fly. He said, "I knew I would get it done." The home run was a bonus, not to mention historic. Whose dramatic heroics punched the Dodgers postseason ticket in 2004?

a) Steve Finley
b) Adrian Beltre
c) Shawn Green
d) Robin Ventura

Q70: On October 20, 1988, the Dodgers clinched the World Series with a 5-2 victory over the Oakland Athletics. That championship club still inspires us to dream, but what came after was fifteen years of postseason misses and heartaches. LA didn't return to the playoffs until 1995 when the Dodgers were swept from the NLDS by the Cincinnati Reds. The Atlanta Braves swept the Dodgers from the NLDS in 1996. Then followed another long stretch with no October baseball at Chavez Ravine. Finally, the club won 93 games and a division title in 2004, but after the grand slam heroics vs. the Giants to end the regular season, the Dodgers quickly fell into a two-game hole vs. the St. Louis Cardinals in the NLDS. Were the Dodgers really destined for a third postseason sweep in a decade? It felt almost inevitable, but this pitcher didn't care. With the postseason dreams of a city firmly on his shoulders, this journeyman starter pitched the game of his life—a five-hit shutout to break the Dodgers eight-game, fifteen-year postseason skid against a Cardinals offense that scored a league-best 855 runs in the regular season. Which pitcher won Game 3 of the 2004 NLDS for the Dodgers?

a) Wilson Alvarez
b) Jose Lima
c) Odalis Perez

d) Jeff Weaver

TOP OF THE FOURTH
ANSWER KEY

61: b. Mike Davis.

62: a. Tony La Russa.

63: d. Mel Didier.

64: c. Mickey Hatcher.

65: a. Bob Welch.

66: b. Jerry Reuss.

67: d. Rick Monday.

68: b. 11.

69: a. Steve Finley.

70: b. Jose Lima.

BOTTOM OF THE FOURTH

Q71: In Game 2 of the 2009 NLDS vs. the St. Louis Cardinals, the Dodgers offense was held in check by Cards ace Adam Wainwright for eight innings. Wainwright gave up just three hits and one run—a long fourth inning home run to Andre Ethier. But manager Tony La Russa lifted Wainwright for a pinch-hitter in the top of the ninth, and looked to lefty-righty tandem Trever Miller and Ryan Franklin to close out the Dodgers in the home half of the frame. It was a great move for two-plus batters. An infield pop fly and a lazy fly ball to center saw the Dodgers down to their last out ... but a miscue by left fielder Matt Holliday turned a sinking line drive into a two-base error, and gave life to the home crowd. A walk followed by a single tied the game, and another walk set the stage for some pinch-hit heroics. Who won Game 2 of the 2009 NLDS with a dramatic pinch-hit, walk-off single?
  a) Ronnie Belliard
  b) Jim Thome
  c) Orlando Hudson
  d) Mark Loretta

Q72: The 1988 NLCS vs. the New York Mets featured the first-ever Game 7 in Dodger Stadium history. Who pitched a complete-game shutout to win that Game 7 and clinch the pennant for the Dodgers?
  a) Tim Leary
  b) Tim Belcher
  c) Orel Hershiser
  d) John Tudor

Q73: This Dodger had a .171 average against phenom Dwight Gooden in 72 career at-bats. However, it's one at-bat vs. Gooden during Game 4 of the 1988 NLCS that really counts. With the Dodgers trailing the Mets 4-2 in the ninth inning, he launched a game-tying, two-run home run that sent the game to extra-innings. Whose late game heroics turned the series around and propelled the Dodgers to the pennant?

   a) Mike Scioscia
   b) Kirk Gibson
   c) Danny Heep
   d) John Shelby

Q74: Game 4 of the 1988 NLCS featured even more late-inning heroics. Who hit a game-winning home run with two outs in the 12th inning to even the series at two games apiece?

   a) Mike Scioscia
   b) Kirk Gibson
   c) Danny Heep
   d) John Shelby

Q75: In the strike-shortened 1981 season, Yankee Ron Guidry was 11-5 in 23 starts. He posted a league-best .992 WHIP in 127 innings, which is a ridiculously low number for a starter known for being a workhorse. He also gave up just 12 home runs in the regular season. Add the pressure of the postseason to the mix, and it's easy to recognize how difficult a task the Dodgers faced when Guidry took the mound for Game 5 of the World Series. Guidry cruised through six innings. He gave up just two hits and no runs. But in the seventh, with the Dodgers trailing 1-0 and facing the prospect of traveling back to the Bronx down three games to two, something special happened: back-to-back home runs against one of baseball's premier pitchers. The Dodgers won 2-1, and later would close out the series with a Game 6 victory. Which Dodgers did this historic feat?

   a) Pedro Guerrero and Steve Yeager
   b) Steve Garvey and Ron Cey
   c) Ken Landreaux and Dusty Baker
   d) Davey Lopes and Bill Russell

Q76: Sandy Koufax took the mound for Game 7 of the 1965 World Series vs. Jim Kaat and the Minnesota Twins. The home team had won every game in the series and Game 7 was at Metropolitan Stadium. But Koufax did the job on the mound: complete game, 10 strikeouts, three hits, no runs. All he needed was a little help from the offense. And he got it on the strength of a fourth-inning home run that proved to be the game-winner in a 2-0 game. Whose long ball won a world championship for the 1965 Dodgers?
   a) Lou Johnson
   b) Willie Davis
   c) Jim Gilliam
   d) Wes Parker

Q77: The Dodgers and Cardinals were locked in a tight pennant race in 1963 when the clubs met in St. Louis for a critical three-game series. LA won the first two games of the series but faced Bob Gibson—one of the hardest throwers and scariest pitchers on the planet—in the finale. A win would go a long way to securing the pennant, but a loss would give the Cards momentum in the season's final days. Gibson and the Cards built a 5-1 lead through seven innings when the Dodgers sent out a pinch-hitter for his very first major-league at-bat to lead off the eighth inning. He made good contact, but made an out … however, the Dodgers rallied for three runs to cut the deficit to 5-4. The pinch-hitter stayed in the game, and in the ninth inning he got another at-bat. He promptly belted a game-tying home run. The Dodgers would go on to win in 13 innings. The Cards never recovered and the Dodgers closed out the pennant over the next two weeks. Here's the crazy part: the rookie pinch-hitter, who hit a game-tying home run in his second at-bat? It was his only career hit for the Dodgers. Whose lone bomb for the Dodgers helped secure the 1963 pennant?
   a) Marv Breeding
   b) Roy Gleason

c) Dick Nen
d) Derrell Griffith

Q78: The Dodgers would go on to win the 1963 World Series in dominant fashion—a clean sweep. Game 4 was at Dodger Stadium, and it was the first time in stadium history that LA won a postseason clincher at home. Which team did the Dodgers defeat in the 1963 World Series?
   a) Chicago White Sox
   b) New York Yankees
   c) Detroit Tigers
   d) Baltimore Orioles

Q79: Sandy Koufax's Game 7 shutout in the 1965 World Series vs. the Minnesota Twins was the Dodgers third shutout of the series and the second in three games for Koufax, who beat Jim Kaat in Game 5, 7-0. But it was a once-in-a-lifetime performance by another pitcher that gave the Dodgers life in the series. Faced with a two-game hole, this pitcher took the mound in a must-win Game 3 and tossed a complete-game five-hit shutout. It was Koufax who rightfully won Series MVP honors … but who won Game 3 and made Koufax's heroics possible?
   a) Ron Perranoski
   b) Jim Brewer
   c) Don Drysdale
   d) Claude Osteen

Q80: Who won a pennant with a walk-off single vs. Phillies pitcher Tug McGraw in Game 4 of the 1978 NLCS?
   a) Davey Lopes
   b) Rick Monday
   c) Steve Garvey
   d) Bill Russell

BOTTOM OF THE FOURTH
ANSWER KEY

71: d. Mark Loretta.

72: c. Orel Hershiser.

73: a. Mike Scioscia.

74: b. Kirk Gibson.

75: a. Pedro Guerrero and Steve Yeager.

76: a. Lou Johnson.

77: c. Dick Nen.

78: b. New York Yankees.

79: d. Claude Osteen.

80: d. Bill Russell.

"To be good, you've gotta have a lot of little boy in you."
— *Roy Campanella*

5 THE SLUGGERS

In the fifth, it's all about the sluggers. Guys who can hit *bombs*. One sent a ball completely out of Dodger Stadium. Another hit 15 in a *single* month. And yet another hit seven in one season … *as a pinch-hitter*. A handful of Dodgers own home run titles. A slew of Dodgers are on yearly and career leaderboards.

Want bombs in the postseason?
Check.
Bombs that set major-league records?
Check.
Record-setting bombs by rookies?
Check.
The list could go on, and on, and on.
Let's get started.

TOP OF THE FIFTH

Q81: The 1977 Dodgers led the league with 191 home runs—including three by pitcher Rick Rhoden. The Dodgers also had four players with 30 home runs—something that had never happened in major-league history, not even by the vaunted Yankees teams of the 1920s. Which four players hit 30-plus home runs for the 1977 Dodgers?
  a) Ron Cey, Steve Garvey, Rick Monday, Jeffrey Leonard
  b) Steve Garvey, Reggie Smith, Dusty Baker, Lee Lacy
  c) Dusty Baker, Ron Cey, Steve Garvey, Reggie Smith
  d) Rick Monday, Ron Cey, Steve Garvey, Dusty Baker

Q82: The major-league record for home runs in a single month is 20, set by a juiced up Sammy Sosa in June 1998. The franchise record for the Los Angeles Dodgers is 15 home runs in a single month. What slugger holds this record?
  a) Eric Karros
  b) Pedro Guerrero
  c) Matt Kemp
  d) Shawn Green

Q83: A slugger also hit 15 home runs in a single month during the Brooklyn era of Dodger history. What Dodger holds this record?
  a) Gil Hodges
  b) Roy Campanella
  c) Carl Furillo
  d) Duke Snider

Q84: The 30/30 club is an elite group because it requires a combination of power and speed that is one of the rarest and most prized commodities in the game. The first slugger with a 30/30 season for the Dodgers is also the only player in franchise history

with two such seasons. Who is this slugger?
   a) Matt Kemp
   b) Andre Ethier
   c) Raul Mondesi
   d) Gary Sheffield

Q85: The second player in franchise history to post a 30/30 season was the 35th player and 11th fastest in major-league history to reach that milestone—he took just 130 games to amass 30 homers and 30 steals. Who is this slugger?
   a) Matt Kemp
   b) Andre Ethier
   c) Raul Mondesi
   d) Gary Sheffield

Q86: Cody Bellinger made his Dodgers debut on April 25, 2017. It took five games for Bellinger to hit his first bomb. His second bomb came in his very next at-bat, and it was also the second of three consecutive ninth inning home runs as the Dodgers rallied for an unbelievable 6-5 victory vs. the Phillies. In just 132 games, Bellinger would go on to smash 39 home runs—including six multi-home run games—which set both the franchise and National League record for home runs by a rookie. Which slugger previously held the franchise record with 35 home runs during his rookie campaign?
   a) Mike Piazza
   b) Adrian Beltre
   c) Matt Kemp
   d) Eric Karros

Q87: Babe Herman (.678, 1930) and Duke Snider (.647, 1954) own the top two slugging percentages for the Brooklyn era in franchise history. For LA, the best season mark is .643. Who hit 43 home runs in just 141 games for the best slugging percentage in LA history?
   a) Mike Piazza

b) Adrian Beltre
c) Gary Sheffield
d) Shawn Green

Q88: A handful of players led the league in slugging for the Brooklyn Dodgers—most notably Duke Snider, who did it twice, in 1953 and 1956. Through 2017, only one player has ever led the league in slugging for the LA Dodgers. Who is this slugger?
   a) Eric Karros
   b) Pedro Guerrero
   c) Matt Kemp
   d) Shawn Green

Q89: Duke Snider led the league with 43 home runs in 1956. The fact his home run title came during the era of Aaron, Mays, Banks, Mathews and Kiner makes it even more impressive. Through 2017, only two players have won home run titles for the LA Dodgers. Who are these sluggers?
   a) Shawn Green/Matt Kemp
   b) Adrian Beltre/Shawn Green
   c) Matt Kemp/Adrian Beltre
   d) Gary Sheffield/Shawn Green

Q90: Duke Snider led the league in total bases three times—including back-to-back seasons in 1953-54—but only one LA Dodger has ever led the league in total bases. In 161 games, this slugger had 195 hits, 33 doubles, four triples, and he led the league with 39 home runs and 353 total bases. He won two-thirds of the Triple Crown and placed second in league MVP balloting. Who is this slugger?
   a) Shawn Green
   b) Gary Sheffield
   c) Adrian Beltre
   d) Matt Kemp

TOP OF THE FIFTH
ANSWER KEY

81: c. Dusty Baker, Ron Cey, Steve Garvey, Reggie Smith.

82: b. Pedro Guerrero.

83: d. Duke Snider.

84: c. Raul Mondesi.

85: a. Matt Kemp.

86: a. Mike Piazza.

87: c. Gary Sheffield.

88: b. Pedro Guerrero.

89: c. Matt Kemp/Adrian Beltre.

90: d. Matt Kemp.

BOTTOM OF THE FIFTH

Q91: Florida Marlins shortstop Hanley Ramirez had six multi-home run games over two seasons from 2007 to 2008. After Ramirez, the next shortstop with as many as six multi-home run games in a two-year span did so for the Los Angeles Dodgers. Who is this hard-hitting middle infielder?
 a) Jimmy Rollins
 b) Corey Seager
 c) Hanley Ramirez
 d) Rafael Furcal

Q92: To be part of Dodger history is an impressive feat for any player. But, to be labeled as "the very first player in Dodger history to …" is in a different stratosphere altogether. This slugger was the very first player in Dodger history to have back-to-back seasons above .300, with at least 30 home runs, 100 RBIs, 100 walks, and 100 runs. Who achieved this extraordinary feat?
 a) Matt Kemp
 b) Gary Sheffield
 c) Shawn Green
 d) Adrian Beltre

Q93: Arizona Diamondbacks catcher Chris Iannetta had a game in September 2017 in which he had two home runs and eight RBIs. It was just the second time in a decade that a big-league catcher had such a prodigious offensive performance. Who had a 4-for-4, two home run, eight RBIs game as catcher for the Dodgers?
 a) Russell Martin
 b) A.J. Ellis
 c) Yasmani Grandal
 d) Rod Barajas

Q94: In 1932, Johnny Frederick—an outfielder whose career was cut short by leg injuries, and a member of the Pacific Coast League Hall of Fame—set a major-league record with six pinch-hit home runs for the Brooklyn Dodgers. Who set a new major-league record with seven pinch-hit home runs in a single season for the Los Angeles Dodgers?
    a) Jeff Kent
    b) Manny Mota
    c) Jose Morales
    d) Dave Hansen

Q95: In what should have been a Hall of Fame career that was subsequently marred by PEDs, former Dodgers hitting coach Mark McGwire set a major-league record with one home run every 10.61 at-bats. The Dodgers franchise record is one home run every 14.5 at bats. Which slugger holds this record?
    a) Mike Piazza
    b) Shawn Green
    c) Duke Snider
    d) Gary Sheffield

Q96: The franchise record for home runs in a single season is 49. The slugger who set this mark had one of the best offensive seasons in league history—he batted .297 with 125 RBIs, 121 runs, and 370 total bases—yet he didn't lead the league in a single category, and only placed sixth in league MVP balloting. Who is this slugger?
    a) Matt Kemp
    b) Gary Sheffield
    c) Shawn Green
    d) Adrian Beltre

Q97: Babe Herman had a season in Brooklyn in which he amassed 416 total bases. Duke Snider had a career best 378 total bases for Brooklyn in 1954. The LA record is 376. Who won a home run title

on his way to setting an LA era franchise record for total bases in a season?
   a) Mike Piazza
   b) Matt Kemp
   c) Shawn Green
   d) Adrian Beltre

Q98: This slugger singlehandedly carried the Dodgers into the 2008 postseason. He was so prolific down the stretch that the Dodgers' website at MLB.com calls his performance "the most amazing two months of offense the Dodgers have ever seen." Who batted .396 with 17 home runs and 53 RBIs during the final two months of 2008?
   a) Nomar Garciaparra
   b) Manny Ramirez
   c) Matt Kemp
   d) Andre Ethier

Q99: Who was the first Dodger to ever hit a home run completely out of Dodger Stadium?
   a) Duke Snider
   b) Mike Piazza
   c) Mike Marshall
   d) Franklin Stubbs

Q100: This two-time world champion ranks among the top ten in franchise history in numerous categories—games, at bats, runs, hits, total bases, doubles, triples, RBIs, stolen bases—and is one of just three players to score 1,000 runs and collect 2,000 hits for the Dodgers. Who is this extraordinary player?
   a) Carl Furillo
   b) Dixie Walker
   c) Mike Marshall
   d) Willie Davis

BOTTOM OF THE FIFTH
ANSWER KEY

91: b. Corey Seager.

92: b. Gary Sheffield.

93: c. Yasmani Grandal.

94: d. Dave Hansen.

95: d. Gary Sheffield.

96: c. Shawn Green.

97: d. Adrian Beltre.

98: b. Manny Ramirez.

99: b. Mike Piazza.

100: d. Willie Davis.

"Career highlights? I had two. I got an intentional walk from Sandy Koufax and I got out of a rundown against the Mets."
— *Bob Uecker*

6 THE HURLERS

In the sixth, it's all about the hurlers. Guys who can paint the corners and throw gas. One earned the first official save in major-league baseball ... *and* threw a no-hitter. Another had 18 strikeouts in a game.

Twice.

And yet another began his career in such spectacular fashion that only *three* other pitchers in major-league history can match his numbers.

The Cy Young Award feels right at home in LA.

ERA and strikeout titles?

Think Blue.

League-leading victory totals?

Think Blue.

Dominant closers?

Think Blue.

This list could also go on, and on, and on.

Let's get started.

TOP OF THE SIXTH

Q101: This pitcher was the first in major-league history to record an official save when the new rule went into effect on Opening Day 1969. Ironically, it was his only relief outing the entire season. He would win 20 games and make his first All-Star team that same year—and one year later, he became the first Los Angeles Dodger not named Sandy Koufax to pitch a no-hitter. Who achieved these fantastic feats?
    a) Alan Foster
    b) Bill Singer
    c) Sandy Vance
    d) Joe Moeller

Q102: Sandy Koufax set a franchise record when he struck out 18 San Francisco Giants on August 31, 1959. He tied his own record with 18 Ks vs. the Chicago Cubs on April 24, 1962. Who tied Koufax's record with 18 Ks vs. the Atlanta Braves?
    a) Clayton Kershaw
    b) Fernando Valenzuela
    c) Zack Greinke
    d) Ramon Martinez

Q103: This Dodger pitched a no-hitter on the same day his former teammate Dave Stewart pitched a no-hitter for the Oakland Athletics. It was the first time in baseball's modern era that two no-hitters occurred on the same day. Tommy Lasorda said, "It couldn't have happened to a tougher, more competitive guy." Who tossed a no-hitter vs. the St. Louis Cardinals on June 29, 1990?
    a) Mike Morgan
    b) Ramon Martinez
    c) Fernando Valenzuela
    d) Tim Belcher

Q104: In just three seasons this pitcher had 81 saves for the Dodgers—and he converted a major-league record 47 of his first 50 career save opportunities. Who is this lights-out closer?
   a) Takashi Saito
   b) Tom Niedenfuer
   c) Jonathan Broxton
   d) Jay Howell

Q105: In 2017, Tampa Bay Rays rookie Jacob Faria became just the fourth pitcher in major-league history to win his first three big-league starts while amassing 20-plus strikeouts and issuing fewer than five walks. Russ Ford did it for the Yankees in 1910. Mel Queen did it for the Reds in 1967. And ... who did it for the Los Angeles Dodgers?
   a) Clayton Kershaw
   b) Orel Hershiser
   c) Fernando Valenzuela
   d) Bob Welch

Q106: The Braves were the first franchise in major-league history to boast four pitchers with 2,000-plus strikeouts: Warren Spahn, Phil Niekro, John Smoltz, and Tom Glavine. The Dodgers became the second when Clayton Kershaw struck out Milwaukee's Jonathan Villar in the second inning of his June 2017 start at Miller Park. Kershaw joined Sandy Koufax, Don Drysdale, and Don Sutton in the Dodgers 2,000-K club. Which of these four aces recorded 2,000 strikeouts without ever leading the league in Ks?
   a) Clayton Kershaw
   b) Sandy Koufax
   c) Don Drysdale
   d) Don Sutton

Q107: Clayton Kershaw had 14 strikeouts in just seven innings of work vs. Milwaukee in the contest that saw him record his 2,000th K. LA's bullpen tallied another 12 strikeouts in five scoreless innings for

a major-league tying (and new National League record) 26 Ks. Another record was set that night. This Dodgers reliever recorded his 36th strikeout of the season, but had not yet issued a single walk. Which pitcher began 2017 with such pinpoint accuracy?
   a) Josh Fields
   b) Luis Avilan
   c) Kenley Jansen
   d) Pedro Baez

Q108: Only one Dodgers pitcher has recorded seven or more seasons with 200-plus strikeouts. Who holds this franchise record?
   a) Clayton Kershaw
   b) Sandy Koufax
   c) Don Drysdale
   d) Don Sutton

Q109: In 2017, Clayton Kershaw was 14-2 with a 2.18 ERA at the All-Star break. He also had a ratio of 10.8 strikeouts per nine innings. He became just the fourth pitcher in major-league history to reach the break with 14 wins, an ERA below 2.50, and at least 10 strikeouts per nine innings. The group also includes Hall of Famers Pedro Martinez (1999) and Randy Johnson (2000). The final member of that group did it in a Dodgers uniform. Who is the fourth member of this elite group of pitchers?
   a) Orel Hershiser
   b) Sandy Koufax
   c) Bob Welch
   d) Don Drysdale

Q110: Kenley Jansen made his major-league debut with the Dodgers in 2010 and was nearly unhittable. In 25 games and 27 innings out of the bullpen, Jansen gave up just 12 hits and two earned runs for a miniscule 0.67 ERA. He became the full-time closer in 2012, and five years later he was the franchise leader in saves and the first closer in team history to save more than 200 games. Jansen, however, wasn't always a pitcher. The Dodgers drafted Jansen as a position player. Jansen played four years in the minors—and even had one season in which he hit nine home runs—before the Dodgers converted him to a reliever. What position did Jansen originally play in the Dodgers minor league system?

    a) Third base
    b) Shortstop
    c) Right field
    d) Catcher

TOP OF THE SIXTH
ANSWER KEY

101: b. Bill Singer.

102: d. Ramon Martinez.

103: c. Fernando Valenzuela.

104: a. Takashi Saito.

105: c. Fernando Valenzuela.

106: d. Don Sutton.

107: c. Kenley Jansen.

108: a. Clayton Kershaw.

109: b. Sandy Koufax.

110: d. Catcher.

BOTTOM OF THE SIXTH

Q111: This reliever set a major-league record by converting 84 consecutive save opportunities over a three-year period. He also became the first closer in history to save 45-plus games in three consecutive seasons. Who is this stalwart closer?
    a) Kenley Jansen
    b) Eric Gagne
    c) Jeff Shaw
    d) Todd Worrell

Q112: The youngest 20-game winner in major-league history is Dwight Gooden, who won his 20th for the 1985 New York Mets when he was 20 years and nine months old. In franchise history, Ralph Branca was just 21 years and eight months old when he won his 20th game for the 1947 Brooklyn Dodgers. Who is the youngest 20-game winner in the Los Angeles era of franchise history?
    a) Clayton Kershaw
    b) Ramon Martinez
    c) Fernando Valenzuela
    d) Orel Hershiser

Q113: Hideo Nomo joined the Dodgers in 1995 after a successful career in Japan. Nomo was the first Japanese player in the majors since Masanori Murakami in 1965—and he didn't disappoint. Nomo was 13-6 with a 2.54 ERA and a league-best 236 strikeouts. For what team did Nomo play professionally in Japan before "retiring" to join the Dodgers?
    a) Hokkaido Nippon-Ham Fighters
    b) Chiba Lotte Marines
    c) Kintetsu Buffaloes
    d) Yomiuri Giants

Q114: This Dodger was the starting pitcher in the All-Star Game five times—a major-league record shared with Hall of Famers Lefty Gomez and Robin Roberts. He also holds the records for most strikeouts (19) and innings pitched (19 1/3) in the All-Star Game. Who is this Dodger great?
  a) Sandy Koufax
  b) Don Drysdale
  c) Clayton Kershaw
  d) Don Sutton

Q115: Through 2017, who is the only Dodger starting pitcher to be named All-Star Game Most Valuable Player?
  a) Sandy Koufax
  b) Don Drysdale
  c) Clayton Kershaw
  d) Don Sutton

Q116: Fernando Valenzuela made 10 relief appearances as a teenager for the Dodgers in 1980—and he didn't allow a single earned run in 17-plus innings of work. "Fernandomania" officially got underway in 1981, however, when Valenzuela pitched a five-hit shutout on Opening Day vs. the Houston Astros … in a game that Valenzuela wasn't even supposed to pitch. Whose injury made way for Valenzuela to start Opening Day 1981?
  a) Burt Hooton
  b) Bob Welch
  c) Rick Sutcliffe
  d) Jerry Reuss

Q117: The Dodgers won the World Series in Los Angeles for the first time in 1963. It was a drama-filled season, as the Dodgers took over first place in early July, held off the hard-charging Cardinals in September to claim the pennant with a 99-63 record, and then swept the Yankees in the World Series. This success was fueled by pitching.

Sandy Koufax and Don Drysdale are the obvious names ... but the staff was so good in 1963, the Dodgers had a guy in the bullpen with 16 wins, 21 saves, and a 1.67 ERA. Who was the ace of the Dodgers bullpen in 1963?
  a) Larry Sherry
  b) Ed Roebuck
  c) Bob Miller
  d) Ron Perranoski

Q118: Clayton Kershaw led the NL in strikeouts in 2011, 2013, and 2015. Through 2017, who was the last Dodger other than Kershaw to lead the league in strikeouts?
  a) Fernando Valenzuela
  b) Sandy Koufax
  c) Ramon Martinez
  d) Hideo Nomo

Q119: Clayton Kershaw led the NL in wins in 2011, 2014, and 2017. Through 2017, the last time a Dodger other than Kershaw led the league in wins was 2006, when a pair of Dodgers finished in a five-way tie with John Smoltz, Brandon Webb, and Carlos Zambrano. Which duo tied for the league lead with 16 wins in 2006?
  a) Greg Maddux/Chad Billingsley
  b) Derek Lowe/Brad Penny
  c) Aaron Sele/Greg Maddux
  d) Derek Lowe/Chad Billingsley

Q120: Clayton Kershaw led the league in ERA four consecutive seasons from 2011-14. His teammate Zack Greinke snapped the streak in 2015. In 2017, Kershaw won his fifth ERA title. Through 2017, the last time a Dodger other than Kershaw or Greinke led the league in ERA was 2000. Who placed sixth in Cy Young balloting after posting a league-best 2.58 ERA in 2000?
  a) Kevin Brown

b) Chan Ho Park
c) Darren Dreifort
d) Carlos Perez

BOTTOM OF THE SIXTH
ANSWER KEY

111: b. Eric Gagne.

112: b. Ramon Martinez.

113: c. Kintetsu Buffaloes.

114: b. Don Drysdale.

115: d. Don Sutton.

116: d. Jerry Reuss.

117: d. Ron Perranoski.

118: d. Hideo Nomo.

119: b. Derek Lowe/Brad Penny.

120: a. Kevin Brown.

"I don't like your name. From now on, I'm going to call you 'Bulldog.' You're going to act like a bulldog and pitch like a bulldog."
— *Tommy Lasorda, to Orel Hershiser*

7 FANTASTIC FEATS

Howie Bedell had two RBIs in 58 games as a rookie for the Milwaukee Braves in 1962. He didn't don a big-league uniform again until 1968. Just up from the minors, it was Bedell who hit a pinch-hit sacrifice fly to end Don Drysdale's streak of 58 consecutive scoreless innings.

Imagine that.

A record streak brought to an end by the third and final RBI of Bedell's career. But that's baseball. It's why we love this game.

In the seventh we look at Drysdale's streak, plus some no-no's, hitting streaks, and walk-offs …

Let's get started.

TOP OF THE SEVENTH

Q121: Sandy Koufax was the first player in big-league history to pitch four no-hitters—and he did so in four consecutive seasons from 1962-65. The final gem was perfection, literally, and is widely considered the greatest game ever pitched. Koufax beat the Cubs 1-0 even though the Dodgers offense managed just one hit and two base runners. It was enough, as Koufax fanned 14—including the last six batters of the game. As Koufax neared perfection, the timeless Vin Scully said, "There are 29,000 people in the ballpark, and a million butterflies." The 27th batter to face Koufax on that day must have felt a sense of déjà vu—in 1963, he'd made the final out of Koufax's second no-hitter … and now he was the last obstacle between Koufax and a perfect game. For the only time in major-league history, the final out of a no-hitter was a repeat performance for the pitcher and batter. Who was the final out for Sandy Koufax's no-hitter in 1963 and his perfect game in 1965?
   a) Don Kessinger
   b) Don Young
   c) Ron Santo
   d) Harvey Kuenn

Q122: Don Drysdale broke a 55-year-old record when he pitched 58 consecutive scoreless innings in 1968. His own streak would last 20 years until Orel Hershiser rewrote the record book again. Whose streak of 55 consecutive scoreless innings did Drysdale eclipse in 1968?
   a) Walter Johnson
   b) Cy Young
   c) Christy Mathewson
   d) Grover Cleveland Alexander

Q123: Andre Ethier began the 2011 season on fire. He became the

first player in major-league history to hit safely in 24 consecutive games during the month of April—and he got his streak all the way to 30 in early May, just one game short of tying the franchise record. Who had a franchise record 31-game hitting streak for the Dodgers?
  a) Steve Garvey
  b) Willie Davis
  c) Maury Wills
  d) Mike Piazza

Q124: In the top of the third inning of a May 1990 contest vs. the Montreal Expos, Fernando Valenzuela gave up a solo home run to the opposing pitcher. How did he respond? Valenzuela led off the bottom of the third with a bomb of his own to straightaway center. It's a rare feat when opposing pitchers homer against each other in the same game. In baseball history it's happened fewer than 20 times. A month later Valenzuela pitched the 20th no-hitter in franchise history ... and the opposing pitcher Valenzuela traded homers with? He made the record book with Valenzuela again when he signed with the Dodgers and pitched the 21st no-hitter in franchise history. Who no-hit the hated San Francisco Giants in 1992 after trading home runs with Fernando Valenzuela in 1990?
  a) Tom Candiotti
  b) Bob Ojeda
  c) Kevin Gross
  d) Pedro Astacio

Q125: Hideo Nomo began his Dodger career in spectacular fashion. In 1995, he led the league in strikeouts and shutouts on his way to Rookie of the Year honors. From 1995-97, his strikeout totals were 236, 234, and 233—which made Nomo just the second pitcher in big-league history to begin his career with three consecutive seasons of 200-plus strikeouts. The first to do so was Dwight Gooden. In 1996, Nomo had a start that was one of the best in franchise history

… and it wasn't his no-hit game. In his third start of the season, Nomo had 10 strikeouts through five innings. He struck out the side in the fifth and again in the seventh. The opposing 6-7-8 hitters went a combined 0-for-9 with nine strikeouts. Nomo tallied 17 strikeouts on the night—one short of the franchise record—in one of the most electric performances in franchise history. Against which team was Nomo lights-out in April 1996?

    a) Atlanta Braves
    b) Florida Marlins
    c) San Francisco Giants
    d) New York Mets

Q126: A walk-off home run is one of the most thrilling plays in all of sports. This Dodger hit *four* in one season to tie a major-league record. Who achieved this fantastic feat?

    a) Matt Kemp
    b) Mike Piazza
    c) Shawn Green
    d) Andre Ethier

Q127: The player Vin Scully called "the heart and soul of the 'Boys of Summer'" once did something on the diamond that transcended baseball and eclipsed a career's worth of fantastic performances in terms of its significance. In 1947, as ignorant fans spewed racist, hate-filled remarks at Jackie Robinson, this heroic icon stood beside Robinson and put a hand on his shoulder in a gesture of solidarity. Robinson would later recall the moment and say, "He was standing by me … I will never forget it." Who is this Dodger legend?

    a) Eddie Stanky
    b) Gil Hodges
    c) Pee Wee Reese
    d) Duke Snider

Q128: In an April 2017 matchup vs. the Philadelphia Phillies, the

Dodgers trailed 5-2 as the game moved to the bottom of the ninth. But then the Dodgers illustrated why the adage "never leave a ballgame early" is so true ... Yasiel Puig, Cody Bellinger, and Justin Turner began the frame with three consecutive home runs to tie the game. The last time a major-league team had tied a game in the ninth inning with three consecutive home runs ... also the Dodgers, in September 2006. In that game, the Dodgers incredibly hit a record-tying *four* consecutive home runs against the San Diego Padres. Which players accomplished this phenomenal feat?
    a) Bill Mueller, James Loney, Marlon Anderson, Matt Kemp
    b) Andre Ethier, J.D. Drew, Wilson Betemit, Nomar Garciaparra
    c) Nomar Garciaparra, James Loney, J.D. Drew, Bill Mueller
    d) Jeff Kent, J.D. Drew, Russell Martin, and Marlon Anderson

Q129: The Dodgers were just the fourth team in major-league history to hit four consecutive home runs in an inning. And after the Hollywood heroics sent the game into extra frames, it was only fitting that Los Angeles beat San Diego on a walk-off home run. Who completed the historic comeback with a dramatic 10th inning blast?
    a) Nomar Garciaparra
    b) Jeff Kent
    c) James Loney
    d) J.D. Drew

Q130: A number of players won batting titles for the Brooklyn Dodgers—most notably Jackie Robinson, who led the league with a .342 average in 1949. From 1958-2017, however, only one player has ever won a batting title for the Los Angeles Dodgers ... and in fact he won two titles in back-to-back seasons. Who is the only batting champion in LA Dodgers history?
    a) Tommy Davis
    b) Mike Piazza
    c) Steve Garvey

d) Pedro Guerrero

TOP OF THE SEVENTH
ANSWER KEY

121: d. Harvey Kuenn.

122: a. Walter Johnson.

123: b. Willie Davis.

124: c. Kevin Gross.

125: b. Florida Marlins.

126: d. Andre Ethier.

127: c. Pee Wee Reese.

128: d. Jeff Kent, J.D. Drew, Russell Martin, and Marlon Anderson.

129: a. Nomar Garciaparra.

130: a. Tommy Davis.

BOTTOM OF THE SEVENTH

Q131: There have been 12 games in Dodger history in which a player has hit three or more home runs with six or more RBIs. Who is the only Dodger in history to have two such games?
a) Gil Hodges
b) Duke Snider
c) Mike Piazza
d) Shawn Green

Q132: In major-league history, only ten players have had five extra-base hits in a single game. Two of them did it for the Dodgers. Who are they?
a) Duke Snider/Gil Hodges
b) Shawn Green/Steve Garvey
c) Jackie Robinson/Matt Kemp
d) Yasiel Puig/Kirk Gibson

Q133: You know about the insane scoreless inning streaks attained by Don Drysdale and Orel Hershiser ... but do you know the first major-league pitcher in history to start a season with 41 consecutive innings without allowing an earned run?
a) Zack Greinke
b) Clayton Kershaw
c) Fernando Valenzuela
d) Bob Welch

Q134: In 1952, Walt Dropo set a major-league record when he hit safely in 12 consecutive at-bats for the Detroit Tigers. The NL record is 10 and is shared by a handful of players—including one member of the Los Angeles Dodgers. Who hit safely in 10 consecutive at-bats for the Dodgers?
a) Andre Ethier

b) Shawn Green
c) Matt Kemp
d) Mike Piazza

Q135: The major-league record for stolen bases in a single game is six. Who stole a franchise record five bases in a single game for the Dodgers?
 a) Steve Sax
 b) Maury Wills
 c) Davey Lopes
 d) Willie Davis

Q136: Hall of Fame slugger Jim Thome retired in 2012 with a major-league record 13 career walk-off home runs. Three different players hit a franchise record seven walk-off home runs for the Dodgers. Gil Hodges and Duke Snider both hit seven total between Brooklyn and Los Angeles. The third member of the group hit all seven in LA. Who is the slugger that achieved this fantastic feat?
 a) Pedro Guerrero
 b) Ron Cey
 c) Andre Ethier
 d) Matt Kemp

Q137: Only two players in major-league history have hit three career walk-off grand slams: Vern Stephens and Alex Rodriguez. From 1958-2017, the Dodgers have hit a total of nine walk-off grand slams. Two of them were hit by the same player. Who is the only player in franchise history to hit two walk-off grand slams?
 a) Davey Lopes
 b) Russell Martin
 c) Nomar Garciaparra
 d) Steve Finley

Q138: Nolan Ryan, Mario Soto, Mike Scott, and Dwight Gooden are just a few of the big-name pitchers who dominated the 1980s. However, a Dodger won more games that decade than any other pitcher in the NL. Who won 128 games in the 1980s?

    a) Bob Welch
    b) Orel Hershiser
    c) Jerry Reuss
    d) Fernando Valenzuela

Q139: Zack Wheat scored at least one run in a franchise record 13 consecutive games in 1925. From 1958-2017, the longest such streak for the Dodgers is 12 games. In June 2010, this player scored 17 runs in a 12-game streak that included at least one run per game. He also amassed 24 hits, eight extra-base hits, 15 RBIs, and four stolen bases. Who achieved this extraordinary feat?

    a) James Loney
    b) Matt Kemp
    c) Rafael Furcal
    d) Andre Ethier

Q140: The Dodgers hit a franchise record 23 postseason home runs in 2017. Justin Turner led the way with four bombs while utilityman Enrique Hernandez had three in one game. Cody Bellinger became the youngest-ever Dodger to hit a postseason home run. Corey Seager held the previous record for all of one year. Only two players have ten or more career postseason home runs for the Dodgers. The record is 11, though it seems destined to fall in this era of expanded playoffs. Through 2017, who is the franchise leader with 11 career postseason home runs?

    a) Gil Hodges
    b) Ron Cey
    c) Duke Snider
    d) Steve Garvey

BOTTOM OF THE SEVENTH
ANSWER KEY

131: d. Shawn Green.

132: b. Shawn Green/Steve Garvey.

133: c. Fernando Valenzuela.

134: a. Andre Ethier.

135: c. Davey Lopes.

136: c. Andre Ethier.

137: a. Davey Lopes.

138: d. Fernando Valenzuela.

139: c. Rafael Furcal.

140: c. Duke Snider.

"He [Jackie Robinson] was the greatest competitor I've ever seen. I've seen him beat a team with his bat, his glove, his feet, and in a game in Chicago one time, with his mouth."
— *Duke Snider*

8 AWARD WINNERS

Whitey Herzog famously said, "We need just two players to be a contender: Babe Ruth and Sandy Koufax."

It's a funny line.

It also underscores a significant truth: baseball is a team game. Even Herzog, in his jest, said *contender*. If you want to be a champion, then you need a team.

You don't build a franchise as successful as the Dodgers unless the franchise culture embraces that simple fact.

But, the hardware *is* nice.

In the eighth, the trivia is all about award-winning Dodgers.

TOP OF THE EIGHTH

Q141: In 2017, Cody Bellinger became the 18th player in franchise history to win Rookie of the Year honors—and if the Dodgers had won Game 7 of the World Series vs. the Houston Astros, then he would have been just the third player to win top rookie honors and a world championship in the same season. Which two players actually did win top rookie honors and a world championship in the same season?
    a) Rick Sutcliffe/Steve Howe
    b) Fernando Valenzuela/Jim Lefebvre
    c) Frank Howard/Ted Sizemore
    d) Steve Sax/Jackie Robinson

Q142: In 1930, rookie slugger Wally Berger hit 38 home runs for the Boston Braves—including 21 in his first 55 games. Berger was the fastest rookie in history to reach 21 home runs … until this Dodgers Rookie of the Year recipient. Who belted 21 home runs in his first 51 games—including a record five multi-homer games—during his award-winning rookie season with the Dodgers?
    a) Frank Howard
    b) Eric Karros
    c) Mike Piazza
    d) Cody Bellinger

Q143: Who is the only shortstop in franchise history to win the Gold Glove Award in back-to-back seasons?
    a) Cesar Izturis
    b) Alfredo Griffin
    c) Bill Russell
    d) Maury Wills

Q144: In 1955, the Dodgers won the first world championship in

franchise history thanks to this pitcher, who shutout the Yankees 2-0, on the road, in Game 7 of the World Series. For his heroics, who won 1955 World Series MVP honors?
   a) Johnny Podres
   b) Don Newcombe
   c) Carl Erskine
   d) Billy Loes

Q145: In 1956, this pitcher won a league-best 27 games as the Dodgers won a fourth pennant in five seasons. For his efforts, he became the first player in major-league history to win both the Cy Young Award and Most Valuable Player Award in the same season. Who achieved this extraordinary feat?
   a) Sal Maglie
   b) Don Newcombe
   c) Carl Erskine
   d) Sandy Koufax

Q146: In 2014, it was Clayton Kershaw who won both Cy Young and Most Valuable Player honors for the Dodgers. The dominant lefty said afterward, "Individual awards aren't why we play this game, but I definitely don't take this honor lightly, especially being a pitcher and winning the MVP. It's pretty awesome." In just 27 starts, Kershaw tied his previous career high for victories. How many games did Kershaw win in 2014?
   a) 19
   b) 20
   c) 21
   d) 22

Q147: Through 2017, a Dodger has won Rookie of the Year honors an incredible 18 times. That dominance of the ROY goes back to its inception. Who won the first Rookie of the Year Award in major-league history?

a) Don Newcombe
b) Joe Black
c) Jackie Robinson
d) Jim Gilliam

Q148: Four Dodgers have won All-Star Game Most Valuable Player honors … and one of them actually won the award twice. Through 2017, who is the only player in franchise history to twice be named MVP of the All-Star Game?
a) Steve Garvey
b) Mike Piazza
c) Don Sutton
d) Maury Wills

Q149: This pitcher was known for a knuckle curve that he developed as a kid—accidentally—while trying to imitate Hoyt Wilhelm's famous knuckleball. It served him well. In the 1981 postseason, he won two elimination games, NLCS MVP honors, and the title-clinching Game 6 of the World Series. Who is this award-winning pitcher?
a) Burt Hooton
b) Bobby Castillo
c) Jerry Reuss
d) Bob Welch

Q150: This pitcher was a minor-leaguer in July 1959. Three months later he was World Series MVP. In four games out of the bullpen, he pitched 12 2/3 innings and gave up just one run vs. the Chicago White Sox. He earned two saves and two wins—including the deciding Game 6, when he pitched 5 2/3 scoreless innings. Who was the MVP of the 1959 World Series?
a) Stan Williams
b) Johnny Klippstein
c) Clem Labine

d) Larry Sherry

TOP OF THE EIGHTH
ANSWER KEY

141: b. Fernando Valenzuela/Jim Lefebvre.

142: d. Cody Bellinger.

143: d. Maury Wills.

144: a. Johnny Podres.

145: b. Don Newcombe.

146: c. 21.

147: c. Jackie Robinson.

148: a. Steve Garvey.

149: a. Burt Hooton.

150: d. Larry Sherry.

BOTTOM OF THE EIGHTH

Q151: Only two players in Los Angeles Dodgers history have ever had 30 home runs and 200 hits in a season. The first player to achieve this remarkable feat was second in league MVP balloting ... however, he did win his fifth consecutive Silver Slugger Award. Who is this award-winning Dodger?
  a) Shawn Green
  b) Steve Garvey
  c) Adrian Beltre
  d) Mike Piazza

Q152: The second player in franchise history with 30 home runs and 200 hits also placed second in league MVP balloting ... and won his first career Silver Slugger Award. Who is this award-winning Dodger?
  a) Shawn Green
  b) Steve Garvey
  c) Adrian Beltre
  d) Mike Piazza

Q153: Sandy Koufax owns four of the top five strikeout totals in franchise history—including the top three spots, which came during his Cy Young seasons (382, 1965; 317, 1966; 306, 1963). Only one other Cy Young winner in franchise history has posted 300 strikeouts in a season ... though ironically, his strikeout title and Cy Young Award were in different seasons. Which Cy Young winner also has a 300-K season for the Dodgers?
  a) Don Newcombe
  b) Don Drysdale
  c) Fernando Valenzuela
  d) Clayton Kershaw

Q154: Tommy Lasorda was a two-time Manager of the Year winner

(1983, 1988). Who is the only other manager in Los Angeles Dodgers history to win this prestigious award?
  a) Don Mattingly
  b) Joe Torre
  c) Dave Roberts
  d) Jim Tracy

Q155: The Roberto Clemente Award is one of the most prestigious in the game. Only one player from all of baseball receives the annual award given to the player "who best exemplifies the game of baseball, sportsmanship, community involvement and the individual's contribution to his team." Who was the first player in Los Angeles Dodgers history to receive this honor?
  a) Steve Sax
  b) Mike Scioscia
  c) Steve Garvey
  d) Eric Karros

Q156: The Dodgers are one of only a handful of teams that can boast two winners of the Roberto Clemente Award. Who was the second player in franchise history to receive this honor?
  a) Clayton Kershaw
  b) Mike Piazza
  c) Mike Marshall
  d) Orel Hershiser

Q157: Injuries are inevitable for professional athletes—and even superstars are not immune. It's a testament to a player's character when he reaches the pinnacle of his sport, falls due to injury, and then rebounds to find himself once more at the pinnacle. Who is the only Dodger in history to win the Cy Young Award and then later battle his way back to the top of his game and earn NL Comeback Player of the Year honors?
  a) Clayton Kershaw

b) Orel Hershiser
c) Fernando Valenzuela
d) Mike Marshall

Q158: In 1957, baseball glove manufacturer Rawlings instituted its annual Gold Glove Award to recognize the best fielder at each position. The first-ever Gold Gloves were not separated by leagues—there was only one winner per position for all of baseball. In other words, it was an elite group. Which Dodger won a Gold Glove Award in its inaugural 1957 season?
    a) Gil Hodges
    b) Charlie Neal
    c) Wally Moon
    d) Wes Parker

Q159: Through 2017, third base is the only position at which no Dodger has ever won a Gold Glove. On the mound, up the middle, behind the dish, first base and the outfield … the Dodgers boast multiple winners and guys who have won multiple times. And of the multiple winners, one particularly stands out for being the first in franchise history to win five consecutive Gold Glove Awards. Who is this stalwart defensive player?
    a) Gil Hodges
    b) Charlie Neal
    c) Wally Moon
    d) Wes Parker

Q160: In Dodger history, a long list of players have won Rookie of the Year honors. Some of them show up on a second list as well—Cy Young winners. Impressive, right? How many times in franchise history has a pitcher won the Rookie of the Year Award and then added—either in the same season or later in their careers—a Cy Young Award to the trophy case?
    a) 1

b) 2
c) 3
d) 4

BOTTOM OF THE EIGHTH
ANSWER KEY

151: d. Mike Piazza.

152: c. Adrian Beltre.

153: d. Clayton Kershaw.

154: c. Dave Roberts.

155: c. Steve Garvey.

156: a. Clayton Kershaw.

157: b. Orel Hershiser.

158: a. Gil Hodges.

159: d. Wes Parker.

160: b. 2 (Don Newcombe, Fernando Valenzuela).

"You may glory in a team triumphant, but you fall in love with a team in defeat. Losing after great striving is the story of man, who was born to sorrow, whose sweetest songs tell of saddest thought, and who, if he is a hero, does nothing in life as becomingly as leaving it."
— *Roger Kahn,* The Boys of Summer

9 THE TEAMS

As we move to the ninth, we take a look at some of the greatest team accomplishments in franchise history. Timely hitting? Absolutely. Dominant pitching? Some of the best in the game.

Major-league records?
Ridiculously long streaks?
Division titles?
World championships?
Think Blue, obviously.

Plus, some pomp and circumstance for Jackie Robinson, Sandy Koufax, and Roy Campanella. All of that, here in the ninth ...

TOP OF THE NINTH

Q161: For the first-ever game at Dodger Stadium, team owner Walter O'Malley's wife, Kay, threw out the ceremonial first pitch. The starting pitcher was Johnny Podres, and the opponent was the Cincinnati Reds. Duke Snider singled in the second inning for the Dodgers first hit in the new ballpark. The Reds spoiled the day, 6-3, but *Times* columnist John Hall wrote, "Los Angeles has itself a major-league ballpark, a truly remarkable stadium that is obviously destined to become recognized as the finest in the world." In which season did Dodger Stadium open?
    a) 1960
    b) 1961
    c) 1962
    d) 1963

Q162: There is just one decade in major-league history in which the Dodgers hit more home runs than any other team. In that same decade the Dodgers also had baseball's top home run hitting duo with 636 combined bombs. In which decade did the Dodgers dominate baseball's slugging leaderboards?
    a) 1940s
    b) 1950s
    c) 1960s
    d) 1970s

Q163: In 1955, the Dodgers led the league with 201 home runs and powered their way to victory in the World Series. In which season were the Dodgers last in the league with 78 home runs ... but still world champions?
    a) 1965
    b) 1981
    c) 1988

d) 1963

Q164: The ceremony in which the Dodgers retired the jersey numbers of legends Jackie Robinson, Sandy Koufax, and Roy Campanella is widely considered to be one of the greatest moments in Dodger Stadium history. In which year did this event take place?
  a) 1969
  b) 1970
  c) 1971
  d) 1972

Q165: The Dodgers hit a franchise record 221 home runs in 2017. It was just the sixth time in franchise history that the club has hit 200-plus bombs in a season. The Dodgers did it three times in five seasons from 2000-04. Which Dodger team was the first in history with 200-plus home runs?
  a) 1951
  b) 1952
  c) 1953
  d) 1954

Q166: The 2017 power surge hit its peak in June when the Dodgers went yard 53 times—the highest single month total in franchise history. In that torrid month, the club tied the 1960 Dodgers for the longest streak of consecutives games with at least one home run. The 2017 Dodgers hit an unbelievable 41 home runs in that streak of … how many games?
  a) 15
  b) 16
  c) 17
  d) 18

Q167: Channel your inner-Maury Wills for this one … in which season did the Los Angeles Dodgers set a franchise record with a

league-best 198 steals?
   a) 1962
   b) 1965
   c) 1983
   d) 1999

Q168: From 1958-2017, the Dodgers have only two seasons with more than 800 runs scored. The first was 1962, when the Dodgers scored a franchise-best 842 runs thanks to an outfield loaded with young talent: Tommy Davis (27 HR, 153 RBIs), Willie Davis (18 HR, 85 RBIs, 32 SB), and Frank Howard (31 HR, 119 RBIs). Up and coming stars Andre Ethier and Matt Kemp were part of the other club to reach this milestone. In which season did the Dodgers score 820 runs for the second highest total in franchise history?
   a) 2006
   b) 2007
   c) 2008
   d) 2009

Q169: The major-league record for consecutive shutouts by a pitching staff is five. It's been done three times: twice by the Baltimore Orioles (1974, 1995), and once by the St. Louis Cardinals (1963). The franchise record for the Dodgers is four consecutive shutouts in 1966. Even more impressive is the fact the shutouts came on the heels of a potentially devastating September loss to San Francisco as the Dodgers were battling the Giants and Pirates for the NL pennant. LA responded by sweeping its next series in historic fashion: 7-0, 1-0, 4-0, and 1-0. The pitching staff gave up just 20 hits and six walks in 37 innings. LA would go on to win eight straight—a streak that propelled the Dodgers from third place to National League champions. Which team did the Dodgers blank in four consecutive games in 1966?
   a) Houston Astros

b) Atlanta Braves
c) Pittsburgh Pirates
d) Philadelphia Phillies

Q170: The longest winning streak in history against one opponent is a staggering 16 games. Which opponent suffered at the hands of the Dodgers for 16 consecutive games during 1973-74?
a) San Francisco Giants
b) Atlanta Braves
c) New York Mets
d) San Diego Padres

TOP OF THE NINTH
ANSWER KEY

161: c. 1962.

162: b. 1950s (Duke Snider, Gil Hodges).

163: a. 1965.

164: d. 1972.

165: c. 1953.

166: c. 17.

167: a. 1962.

168: a. 2006.

169: a. Houston Astros.

170: d. San Diego Padres.

LOS ANGELES DODGERS IQ

BOTTOM OF THE NINTH

Q171: In which decade did the Dodgers win an NL-best 825 games and two world championships?
   a) 1950s
   b) 1960s
   c) 1970s
   d) 1980s

Q172: In which decade did the Dodgers win two world championships and a franchise record 913 games?
   a) 1950s
   b) 1960s
   c) 1970s
   d) 1980s

Q173: The most wins in a decade for the Los Angeles Dodgers is 910. That number could soon change. From 2010-17, the Dodgers won 721 games against 574 losses. That's more wins this decade than any other NL team … though just barely. The St. Louis Cardinals won 720 games, while the Washington Nationals won 704 and the San Francisco Giants were fourth with 671 victories. It'll take two more sensational seasons on the heels of 2017, but the Dodgers need just 189 wins in 2018-19 to set a new mark for wins in a decade. As for the current record … in which decade did the Dodgers win three pennants and an LA era record 910 games?
   a) 1960s
   b) 1970s
   c) 1980s
   d) 1990s

Q174: The longest home winning streak in Dodger Stadium history is 13 games. It's been done twice. The first time was 1993, when the

Dodgers won 13 straight in May and June. The second time was special because it was also the first 13 home games of the season. Which season did the Dodgers begin in record-setting fashion?
   a) 2006
   b) 2009
   c) 2012
   d) 2015

Q175: The Houston Astros began 2017 with a leadoff home run on Opening Day. The Astros closed out 2017 as world champions. It was just the second time in big-league history that one team accomplished both feats in the same season. In what year did the Los Angeles Dodgers become the first major-league team to accomplish this feat?
   a) 1963
   b) 1965
   c) 1981
   d) 1988

Q176: The 2013 Dodgers were in last place from the second week of the season until July 2. At one point the club was 12 games under .500 and 9 1/2 games out of first. But, not only did the Dodgers recover to win the division, an unprecedented hot streak propelled the club to win the division title by *11 games* over the Arizona Diamondbacks. The club's hot streak included the longest road-winning streak in the National League since 1957. How many consecutive road games did the Dodgers win in July and August 2013?
   a) 13
   b) 15
   c) 17
   d) 19

Q177: In 2020, Dodger Stadium will host the All-Star Game for only the second time in its history. Davey Lopes, Reggie Smith, Steve Garvey, and Bill Russell were all in the starting lineup the first time Dodger Stadium hosted the All-Star Game, as a sellout crowd of 56,088 witnessed the unveiling of the Dodger DiamondVision Board and a 4-2 victory for the NL. When did Dodger Stadium host the All-Star Game for the first time?

    a) 1978
    b) 1979
    c) 1980
    d) 1981

Q178: The 2020 All-Star Game will be the second played at Dodger Stadium, but it will be the fourth hosted by the Dodgers. The first was at Ebbets Field and it is noteworthy for also being the first-ever All-Star Game for baseball legend Jackie Robinson. When did Jackie Robinson play his first All-Star Game at Ebbets Field?

    a) 1948
    b) 1949
    c) 1950
    d) 1951

Q179: Steve Sax was a three-time All-Star during eight seasons with the Dodgers from 1981-88. He also made history when he started a game alongside his brother, outfielder/catcher Dave Sax. For which team did Steve and Dave Sax become the first-ever brothers to start a game for the Dodgers?

    a) 1982
    b) 1983
    c) 1984
    d) 1985

Q180: Hall of Fame manager Walter Alston led the Dodgers for 23 successful years. His teams won seven pennants, four World Series titles, and a franchise record 2,040 regular season games. In what

season did Tommy Lasorda take over managerial duties for Walter Alston?
- a) 1975
- b) 1976
- c) 1977
- d) 1978

BOTTOM OF THE NINTH
ANSWER KEY

171: d. 1980s.

172: a. 1950s.

173: b. 1970s.

174: b. 2009.

175: d. 1988.

176: b. 15.

177: c. 1980.

178: b. 1949.

179: b. 1983.

180: c. 1977.

> "Guys ask me, don't I get burned out? How can you get burned out doing something you love? I ask you, have you ever got tired of kissing a pretty girl?"
> — *Tommy Lasorda*

10 EXTRA INNINGS

There is no clock in baseball. You have to get 27 outs, and then you can go home. That's why you never leave a game early. You just don't know what's going to happen next.

But sometimes 27 outs isn't enough.

It's free baseball, and it could go all night. Tense. Exhilarating. And conventional wisdom is tossed. Everything is on the table, because all it takes to win is a single run.

That's why here in extras we've got a bit of everything trivia-wise: base-stealers, longevity and loyalty, some digs at the Giants, and some of the biggest Hall of Fame—and future HOF—names in franchise history.

Finish strong …

TOP OF THE TENTH

Q181: Maury Wills is the franchise leader with 490 career stolen bases. He was also caught stealing a franchise record 171 times. His success rate—74.13—ranks just inside the top 15 in franchise history. The highest success rate in franchise history is 83.10. Who was the Dodgers most successful base stealer?
   a) Delino DeShields
   b) Juan Pierre
   c) Davey Lopes
   d) Dave Roberts

Q182: The 1980s was one of the most successful decades in franchise history. A lot of that success can be attributed to two players. Which duo are the only players to suit up for the Dodgers during every season of the decade that was the 1980s?
   a) Mike Marshall/Mariano Duncan
   b) Pedro Guerrero/Alejandro Pena
   c) Bob Welch/Charlie Hough
   d) Mike Scioscia/Fernando Valenzuela

Q183: Yasmani Grandal hit 65 home runs for the Dodgers during his first three seasons with the club from 2015-17. That total is already the third highest in Los Angeles Dodgers history for a switch-hitter. In fact, a healthy and consistent Grandal could soon become the first-ever Dodger switch-hitter with 100 home runs. Which Dodger hit a franchise record 97 home runs as a switch-hitter?
   a) Todd Hundley
   b) Eddie Murray
   c) Jim Lefebvre
   d) Reggie Smith

Q184: The Dodgers had just two managers in 44 seasons from 1954-

96: Hall of Famers Walter Alston and Tommy Lasorda. In 22 seasons from 1997-2018, how many different managers have led the Dodgers?
  a) 6
  b) 7
  c) 8
  d) 9

Q185: Perhaps even more impressive than the managerial longevity of Walter Alston and Tommy Lasorda is what the Dodgers were able to do behind the dish for better than four decades. From 1948-92 the Dodgers had an unprecedented run of success that featured just four primary backstops: Roy Campanella (1948-57), John Roseboro (1957-67), Steve Yeager (1972-85), and Mike Scioscia (1980-92). Which of these Dodger legends is the franchise leader for games caught?
  a) Roy Campanella
  b) John Roseboro
  c) Steve Yeager
  d) Mike Scioscia

Q186: It's always fun to stumble across stats that make your team's rivals look bad ... which slugger struck out 212 times—the most of any player in major-league history—against Dodgers pitching?
  a) Barry Bonds
  b) Willie Mays
  c) Tony Perez
  d) Willie McCovey

Q187: Who hit a franchise record 130 home runs at Dodger Stadium?
  a) Ron Cey
  b) Steve Garvey
  c) Eric Karros
  d) Matt Kemp

Q188: Through 2017, only ten players in Los Angeles Dodgers history have had a season with 20-plus home runs, 300 total bases, and 90 runs scored. In 1997, Raul Mondesi and Mike Piazza became the first-ever Dodger teammates to do so in the same season. Shawn Green and Gary Sheffield would repeat that feat in 2001. There has only been one hitter in franchise history with three such seasons in Blue. Who is this consistent star?
    a) Matt Kemp
    b) Steve Garvey
    c) Ron Cey
    d) Adrian Beltre

Q189: Through 2017, who is the most recent Dodger with 20-plus home runs, 300 total bases, and 90 runs scored?
    a) Cody Bellinger
    b) Corey Seager
    c) Yasiel Puig
    d) Joc Pederson

Q190: In Los Angeles Dodgers history, only one player had a season in which he had fewer strikeouts than walks *and* hit 40 home runs with 300 total bases, 100 runs scored, and 100 RBIs. From 1958-2017 is a lot of history … who distinguished himself with such incredible stats?
    a) Gary Sheffield
    b) Adrian Beltre
    c) Matt Kemp
    d) Shawn Green

TOP OF THE TENTH
ANSWER KEY

181: c. Davey Lopes.

182: d. Mike Scioscia/Fernando Valenzuela.

183: d. Reggie Smith.

184: c. 8.

185: d. Mike Scioscia.

186: d. Willie McCovey.

187: c. Eric Karros.

188: b. Steve Garvey.

189: b. Corey Seager.

190: a. Gary Sheffield.

BOTTOM OF THE TENTH

Q191: In 1916, Jack Coombs had a perfect 6-0 record vs. the rival New York Giants. Coombs is the only pitcher in Dodger history with six wins in a single season vs. the hated Giants. From 1958-2017, the most wins recorded vs. the Giants in a single season is five—a feat that's been accomplished twice. Who are the only pitchers in Los Angeles Dodgers history to win five games against zero defeats vs. San Francisco in a single season?
    a) Orel Hershiser/Fernando Valenzuela
    b) Don Drysdale/Sandy Koufax
    c) Rick Sutcliffe/Jerry Reuss
    d) Clayton Kershaw/Zack Greinke

Q192: In Brooklyn Dodgers history, two players had seasons in which they hit 10-plus home runs vs. the New York Giants. Which duo accomplished this feat?
    a) Duke Snider/Gil Hodges
    b) Carl Furillo /Jim Russell
    c) Dolph Camilli/Roy Campanella
    d) Pete Reiser/Dixie Walker

Q193: Ron Cey regularly punished the San Francisco Giants. He had 42 career homers against LA's biggest rival—including an LA record-tying eight in 1978. Tommy Davis also hit eight home runs vs. San Fran in 1962. In Los Angeles Dodgers history, who hit a franchise-best 51 career home runs vs. the San Francisco Giants?
    a) Steve Garvey
    b) Eric Karros
    c) Carl Furillo
    d) Gil Hodges

Q194: Braves Hall of Fame legend Warren Spahn beat the San

Francisco Giants a major-league record 56 times in his career. Spahn is at the top of that list, but if you look at the top-ten you'll see five names in Blue. Who beat the San Francisco Giants a franchise-best 34 times during his career?

  a) Don Sutton
  b) Sandy Koufax
  c) Fernando Valenzuela
  d) Don Drysdale

Q195: Today's game rewards power—and no one cares much if that power comes with a lot of swings and misses. It's just the state of the game, something that changes regularly. However, there was a time when plate discipline and power were not mutually exclusive. Who had four seasons with 23-plus home runs *and* more walks than strikeouts?

  a) Ron Cey
  b) Steve Garvey
  c) Pedro Guerrero
  d) Reggie Smith

Q196: The 1968 St. Louis Cardinals pitched 27 shutouts on the season—better than 1-in-4 of their 97 wins. That's an incredible number, and it's the highest in baseball for the past 60 years. The second highest number in that same timeframe belongs to the Los Angeles Dodgers … unfortunately, the club pitched a franchise record 21 shutouts in a season in which the offense was anemic. Which team missed the playoffs despite a franchise best 21 shutouts?

  a) 1972
  b) 1975
  c) 1980
  d) 1982

Q197: Among pitchers with at least 25 starts in a season, whose .875 winning percentage set a franchise record?

a) Alex Wood
b) Orel Hershiser
c) Zack Greinke
d) Clayton Kershaw

Q198: Guys with power usually earn their share of free passes while guys with wheels see a lot of strikes. That's why only once in Los Angeles Dodgers history has a batter hit fewer than 10 home runs in a season *and* drawn 100 free passes. Who hit just two home runs in a season in which he led the league with 108 walks?
a) Dee Gordon
b) Juan Pierre
c) Brett Butler
d) Steve Sax

Q199: In Dodger history, only ten players have had a game with two extra-base hits *and* two stolen bases … and one of those ten accomplished this extremely rare feat *three* times. Who is this Dodger?
a) Maury Wills
b) Steve Sax
c) Yasiel Puig
d) Dee Gordon

Q200: In Dodger history, more than 75 players have hit two triples in the same game … but, only one player has ever had a game with *three* triples. Incidentally, he's also on the list of players with two extra-base hits and two steals in the same game. Who is this Dodger?
a) Maury Wills
b) Steve Sax
c) Yasiel Puig
d) Dee Gordon

BOTTOM OF THE TENTH
ANSWER KEY

191: d. Clayton Kershaw/Zack Greinke.

192: c. Dolph Camilli/Roy Campanella.

193: d. Gil Hodges.

194: d. Don Drysdale.

195: a. Ron Cey.

196: a. 1972.

197: d. Clayton Kershaw.

198: c. Brett Butler.

199: b. Steve Sax.

200: c. Yasiel Puig.

ABOUT THE AUTHOR

Tucker Elliot is a former teacher, coach, and athletic director. He has visited schools on four continents and more than twenty countries as a volunteer or an invited speaker/lecturer. He lives in Florida and Korea. Connect with Tucker on Amazon, Facebook, Twitter, or email: tckrelliot@gmail.com

e-Books by Tucker Elliot

The Day Before 9/11

The Memory of Hope

The Rainy Season

Third Ring Children

The Other Side of the River

Baseball Books by Tucker Elliot

Baltimore Orioles IQ: The Ultimate Test of True Fandom

Cincinnati Reds IQ: The Ultimate Test of True Fandom

Major League Baseball IQ: The Ultimate Test of True Fandom

Tampa Bay Rays IQ: The Ultimate Test of True Fandom

Atlanta Braves IQ: The Ultimate Test of True Fandom

Cleveland Indians IQ: The Ultimate Test of True Fandom

New York Yankees IQ: The Ultimate Test of True Fandom

San Francisco Giants IQ: The Ultimate Test of True Fandom

Washington Nationals IQ: The Ultimate Test of True Fandom

Atlanta Braves: An Interactive Guide to the World of Sports

Boston Red Sox: An Interactive Guide to the World of Sports

San Francisco Giants: An Interactive Guide to the World of Sports

51 Questions for the Diehard Fan: New York Yankees

51 Questions for the Diehard Fan: Atlanta Braves

51 Questions for the Diehard Fan: Baltimore Orioles

BLACK MESA

Visit us on the web to learn more about Black Mesa and our authors:

www.blackmesabooks.com

Or contact us via email:

admin@blackmesabooks.com

SOURCES

Baseball-reference.com (Play Index)

MLB.com (and the official team sites through MLB.com)

BaseballHallofFame.org

ESPN.com

SABR.org

Baseball-Almanac.com

Elias Sports Bureau

www.ingramcontent.com/pod-product-compliance
Lightning Source LLC
Chambersburg PA
CBHW061445040426
42450CB00007B/1223